'I am not aware of any better book on how tl
Lloyd and Cristina Marconi are rigorous, ...,
minded. They are particularly good on how reporting in Brussels has
evolved over the past 20 years.'

Charles Grant, Director, Centre for European Reform

'Europe has common policies but no common politics. It appears only
through the distorting mirror of national media. This pioneering study by
John Lloyd and Cristina Marconi is the first comparative analysis of how
media have covered the EU's biggest crisis since its inception. It offers vital
insight into Europe's differing cultures of communication as well as the
health of its politics.'

Mark Leonard, Director, European Council on Foreign Relations

'A much-needed, well-researched and lively account of the challenge of
covering the EU, this book shows how crucial quality journalism on
European affairs, both from Brussels and from various European capitals,
has become, particularly since the financial crisis.'

Sylvie Kauffmann, Editorial Director, *Le Monde*

RISJ CHALLENGES

CHALLENGES present findings, analysis and recommendations from Oxford's Reuters Institute for the Study of Journalism. The Institute is dedicated to the rigorous, international comparative study of journalism, in all its forms and on all continents. CHALLENGES muster evidence and research to take forward an important argument, beyond the mere expression of opinions. Each text is carefully reviewed by an editorial committee, drawing where necessary on the advice of leading experts in the relevant fields. CHALLENGES remain, however, the work of authors writing in their individual capacities, not a collective expression of views from the Institute.

EDITORIAL COMMITTEE

The editorial advisers on this CHALLENGE were Geert Linnebank and Paul Taylor.

This publication arises from research funded by the John Fell Oxford University Press (OUP) Research Fund.

REPORTING THE EU

NEWS, MEDIA AND THE
EUROPEAN INSTITUTIONS

JOHN LLOYD AND
CRISTINA MARCONI

Published by I.B.Tauris & Co. Ltd in association with
the Reuters Institute for the Study of Journalism, University of Oxford

Published in 2014 by I.B.Tauris & Co. Ltd
6 Salem Road, London W2 4BU
175 Fifth Avenue, New York NY 10010
www.ibtauris.com

Distributed in the United States and Canada Exclusively by Palgrave Macmillan
175 Fifth Avenue, New York NY 10010

ISBN: 978 1 78453 065 5
eISBN: 978 0 85773 740 3

A full CIP record for this book is available from the British Library
A full CIP record is available from the Library of Congress

Library of Congress Catalog Card Number: available

Typeset by Riverside Publishing Solutions, Salisbury, Wiltshire

Printed and bound in Great Britain by T.J. International, Padstow,
Cornwall

Contents

Acknowledgements

The present study takes into account the experiences and points of view expressed by correspondents based in Brussels from seven countries: France, Germany, Greece, Italy, Poland, Spain, and the UK. We interviewed people who have been in the EU capital at different times or who have been covering EU issues from other places, in order to reach a better understanding of the evolution over time of the topic at the centre of our study. We chose people working for different media: print press, TV and radio.

Thanks to the John Fell Oxford University Press (OUP) Research Fund for generous support of the research for this project; the interviewees listed here, and to others who didn't wish to be named; Geert Linnebank and Paul Taylor, for their reading of the draft of this report and their comments on it; those members of the Reuters Institute editorial committee who also read and commented on it; and the staff of the Reuters Institute and of I.B.Tauris for their help in bringing this to publication.

The Interviewees

Anonymous, EU press spokespeople
Hughes Beaudouin, TF1
Ruth Berschens, *Handelsblatt*
Tomasz Bielecki, *Gazeta Wyborcza*
Andrea Bonanni, *La Repubblica*
Jochen Buchsteiner, *Frankfurter Allgemeine Zeitung*
George Candon, FTI (Consultancy)
David Carretta, *Il Foglio*
Vangelis Demeris, freelance (Greece)
Alain Franco, freelance journalist (France)
Federico Fubini, *La Repubblica*

Andrew Gardner, *European Voice*
Luigi Ippolito, *Corriere della Sera*
Matthias Krupa, *Die Zeit*
Anton La Guardia, *The Economist*
Dick Leonard, *The Economist* (formerly)
Karl de Meyer, *Les Echos*
Bernardo de Miguel, *Cinco Dias*
Chris Morris, BBC
John Palmer, *Guardian* (formerly)
Giovanna Pancheri, Sky Italia
George Parker, *Financial Times*
Griselda Pastor, Cadena Ser Radio
Annalisa Piras, Euronews (formerly)
Jean Quatremer, *Libération*
Philippe Ricard, *Le Monde*
Dirk Schuemer, *Frankfurter Allgemeine Zeitung*
Bettina Schulz, *Frankfurter Allgemeine Zeitung* (formerly)
Peter Spiegel, *Financial Times*
Matina Stevis, *Dow Jones-Wall Street Journal*
Paul Taylor, Reuters
Enrico Tibuzzi, ANSA
Toby Vogel, *European Voice*
Bruno Waterfield, *Daily Telegraph*

1

Introduction: Feast and Famine

Commoner: Just think. Which one of these stories do you believe?
Woodcutter: None makes any sense.

(*Rashomon*, Akira Kurosawa, 1950)

The European Union occupies a central position in the politics and economic life of its 28 members and an important one in much of the rest of the world. Few other institutions of governance have such a contested role, and its very existence is increasingly called into question by uncompromising critics, while a growing constituency want it radically reformed. A debate on the legitimacy of the EU's action has always existed and has been quite trenchant in the past, but it has never reached the current level. The EU public has never been so engaged with and opinionated about the EU project as it is now: news media have to take this into account.

It is clearly important that citizens from the 28 EU countries understand what effect the EU Commission, the Parliament, and the Council of Ministers have on their lives – what policies they discuss and approve, what relationship they have with national governments, what assistance they offer to the member states, how much they pay to them, what power they have and what powers they seek to have.

The findings of this study of the journalists whose job it is to cover the institutions of the EU are contradictory. Until the economic crisis hit Europe in the late 2000s, with severe effects on many of the member states and a major threat to the viability of the 14-year-old euro currency used by the 18 member states in the eurozone, most national media covered the EU much less than their own political centres of power, which in some cases meant that they covered it very little. News editors and producers came to view European stories as boring for readerships and viewers. Even after the crisis broke, the coverage remained patchy, and in some cases suffered from a lack of understanding of the issues and mechanisms under discussion, and/or a lack of sufficient staff to give more than a sketch of even critically important issues.

On the other hand, the amount published about and by the European Union is vast. The Union's institutions are lavish with news announcements, with briefings, with prepackaged but often detail-rich interviews with commissioners; think tanks in Brussels and in all the main capitals pour out analyses and advice; the many specialised journals and websites are knowledgeable, up-to-the-minute, and distant enough from their subject to be critical; the global newspapers and wire services continue to support relatively large and active bureaux, whose output enjoys a high reputation.

The problem is with the larger public which is only sporadically interested in politics and public institutions. In times of crisis or of important decisions, the attention reaches a peak, but in good times news coming from Brussels is the first to disappear from newspaper pages and from TV programmes. This seems to us the largest problem facing the news media which have the responsibility of covering the EU: its very structure and mode of operation renders the task of engaging the general European public with it, in journalistic terms, difficult.

Thus 'who cares?' becomes a pertinent question, and the consequences of the general lack of interest in the EU – except at times of crisis, which have brought a more critical, even hostile, attention than before – underpin much of the report's findings. It is first on the list below: but other issues, also set out briefly here and treated in greater detail in the main body of this study, also seem to us to be major ones facing the journalism of the European Union.

A note on the form of this report. It relies on a series of interviews done by the two authors – mainly Cristina Marconi – over a period at the end of 2013 and the first months of 2014. Most of the interviewees are journalists. Though we refer to some of the large academic and expert literature on the EU and the news media, this report is not in the academic tradition.

Who Cares?

The problem of interesting a wide public has different facets.

1. The coverage of the EU is inherently difficult for journalism, above all for broadcasters and for popular papers. Most journalism has long

assumed that it must woo the reader into the story told, since s/he reads or watches, usually, at leisure without any externally imposed need to do so: a few moments of boredom will mean a decision to move on. This is especially true of the most popular news medium, TV.

It is difficult because the Union and its institutions – including, and sometimes most of all, the Parliament – are largely devoid of the dramas, confrontations, rows, large and well-known characters and issues which make up much of the political coverage within the nation states. Instead, the journalists must deal with (changing) officials who are mostly, and remain, unknown to most Europeans. The processes of the Union and especially the Commission are slow, complex, and hard to grasp by a layman; many of the issues handled are technical and detailed; there are constant and often opaque negotiations in the Council of Ministers which brings together departmental ministers and the European Council which unites the heads of state and government of the member states, both of which meet in closed session and retain the largest power.

Even news which significantly impacts on everyday life – a decision which can affect a community in a positive or negative way, and there are many – is delivered in different steps over an extended period, and it can take years before the measures enter into force. If on one hand this shows how carefully every step is taken by the EU authorities, on the other hand it is hard to retain wide interest in the enforcement of a decision taking place years after it has been announced for the first time. The Parliament especially – unlike national assemblies, where the actors are known and the dramas often vivid – has been hard to televise and often soporific. After the May 2014 European elections, with a much increased Eurosceptic representation, the debates have become less tedious, the arguments much fiercer: though the designation 'Eurosceptic' covers a spectrum from anti-euro on economic grounds (the Alternative für Deutschland in Germany) to overtly fascist (Jobbik in Hungary and Golden Dawn in Greece).

2. Popular media – mass-circulation newspapers and television – could in theory do much to convey the central issues being discussed and agreed in the EU to a wide audience. There are two reasons why this is true only to a very limited extent. The most powerful and influential among the European popular newspapers – *Bild* in Germany and the

Daily Mail and the *Sun* in the UK – are strongly critical of the EU or of some aspects of it, take a combative posture vis-à-vis the EU and, especially the UK papers, are accused by the Commission and by many journalist colleagues of distortion and gross inaccuracies. More importantly they – especially the British papers – convey little of the substance of the Union.

However, this press has at times revealed, even if through exaggeration and sometimes falsehood, something of the underlying contradictions and silences of the EU – especially the contradiction between the long-term aim of 'ever closer union' and the reality of continuing national control. Yet a usually confrontational approach, with neither news nor commentary informed by having a permanent correspondent in Brussels, means that polemic and a focus on errors and absurdities is preferred to facts. At the same time, the practised skill with which the popular tabloids present the news means that their message comes through much more powerfully than that of the quality media, influencing voters and public opinion in a way that inevitably has to be taken into account by politicians.

Television coverage is much less polemical – and is legally barred from being so in many European states – but is generally brief. In addition, in nearly every state, the regular habit of watching the news is in decline, especially among the young, with the news accessed when one is interested in specific issues. This might include the EU, but probably only when crises seem imminent.

3. The growing conviction among editors that news about the EU is unpopular with readers and viewers led to a shrinkage, during the 2000s, of the permanent correspondent corps based in Brussels and a greater dependence on coverage from the news media's home base, or from other capitals, such as Paris. EU information depended much more on freelancers and fixers, a less expensive workforce which replaced the established correspondents. In addition, the crisis itself forced further cuts on the news media – leaving the worst-hit countries, which arguably needed the news and analysis the most, with a shrunken representation.

All news is local

Most news organisations, when reporting the EU, produce coverage which is not aimed at Europeans, but at French, Dutch, Polish, and other national citizens. The subtext is: what is the EU doing for, and to, us? Journalists, who find themselves assigned to cover the EU, or 'Europe', thus do what seems to come naturally: they bring their nation with them.

Most journalism from Brussels covers the central institutions of the EU with both eyes on the business of determining how far they act in or against the interests of the home country. To cover it in this fashion is, of course, to miss most of what these institutions do – jerking them into life in print, sound, or images only to judge how far they are useful to the national interest; who are the losers and winners, the opponents and allies; what the national ministers, especially the prime minister, have achieved at their meetings, with the content generally briefed to the national news media representatives by the public relations officials of the government in question. 'Europe' thus becomes an adjunct to the nation, and is simply another chamber in which the latter 'speaks to itself' – or a chamber which each nation can blame when something goes wrong.

The exceptions to this rule are the transnational media – the global wire services, such as Reuters, Bloomberg, AP, and AFP; the global economic papers, such as *The Economist*, the *FT*, and the *Wall Street Journal*; and – to a lesser extent – the global broadcasters, such as the BBC, CNN, and others. These organisations see their mission, and their business model, as providing coverage which has little or no national focus: 'news from nowhere'.

Holding to harsher account

The journalists who covered what became the EU in its first decades were pioneers of a new kind of reporting. Brussels was not only the headquarters of a supranational organisation which had constantly developing powers, but also the crossroads where different journalistic cultures met and worked together on a common project over an indefinite period. In the aftermath of the war, the new correspondents were largely supportive of the organisation and felt they had a role to play in its construction: they saw the institutions through the prism of their founders – Jean Monnet, Paul-Henri Spaak, Altiero Spinelli, and others – who in turn believed that it was a way to stop Europe from again descending into war.

From the 1980s onwards, new generations of journalists adopted a more distant attitude towards the institutions, seeing the Union as a legitimate source of political and economic power which still had to be held to more severe account – whatever their own views were about it. This critical approach deepened and turned harsher in the 2000s, as more evidence emerged of an increasing public disillusionment with the EU in countries, such as France and the Netherlands, where the bulk of the political classes had professed themselves keenly pro-integration. In many cases it became aggressive from 2008, when the EU's most ambitious innovation, the euro currency, demonstrated its fragility and its malign effect – at least in the short term – on (especially) Southern European economies.

As this attitude took firmer hold, the public relations officials charged with communicating with the world via the news media became more embattled and defensive, and were increasingly seen by journalists as overprotective of their masters, and at times unhelpful in explaining the urgent issues of the crisis. The latest moves in terms of economic and financial measures were sometimes developed outside of the EU structures. This marginalisation did not prevent them from trying to convey a strong message on the benefits of the measures taken, even when they were proving largely unpopular in member states. As Hans Magnus Enzensberger puts it in his pamphlet *Brussels, the Gentle Monster*, given the lack of a 'EU public sphere of debate worthy of the name', there has been 'an increasing temptation for the Union to take opinion-shaping in hand for itself'.[1]

The gap in understanding

The economic crisis has significantly altered the work of journalists who cover the EU. It has

- Forced them to keep up with the pace of a decision-making which was highly technical and complex. They had to undergo a steep learning curve and had their relative ignorance exposed. Most were not well versed in economics and finance, and even those who were could hardly understand, at least initially, the new debates, policies, and mechanisms which quickly reached an uncommon degree of complexity. They also had to translate a very complicated message into simple words, given that many of the decisions taken often directly affected their public.

- Encouraged many of them to shift the focus of their reporting from the Brussels/Strasbourg centres to other cities in Europe – especially Athens (for the riots), Berlin (for the decisions), and Frankfurt (for the European Central Bank).
- Widened the gulf between them and the EU, especially the Commission, since it came to seem less relevant to addressing the crisis and its communications were constrained by the market sensitivity of the issues.
- Created a genuine and unprecedented interest among the public looking with concern for fresh and reliable news about new taxes, austerity measures, welfare cuts. Viewers and readers became increasingly demanding, but increasingly sceptical too.

Look what the voters brought in

Journalists covering the EU now see it as undergoing a series of changes unprecedented in its near-sixty-year (since the 1957 Treaty of Rome) history. The strains put upon it by the economic crisis have, at least in the first moment, encouraged many politicians and officials to point the way to 'more Europe' – a much greater fiscal coordination at the centre of the eurozone, both to address the continuing problems in many of the eurozone countries and to give the euro the political backing it has lacked since its invention in 2000. Then, quite abruptly, the political narrative surrounding the EU changed and 'more Europe' became, in many quarters, suspect.

The centrifugal pressures have never been so evident, and the popularity of the anti-EU parties in several countries brought into the Brussels Parliament groups of parties, of the far right and the far left, who agree on one big thing – much 'less Europe' for many, the ideal for most of these being no European Union at all. This happened both in Southern countries as a protest against the austerity measures, and in Northern countries as an expression of the malaise for, as many see it, having to pay for other countries' profligacy.

This means that, for the first time, the European Parliament has the potential for both real drama and a real debate about the most fundamental of issues: the right for the EU to exist. Politicians have been elected who have a reputation for being outspoken and populist, keen on starting controversies and using abrasive language, much more suited to television

7

and popular journalism than the Brussels debate to date. This will represent a temptation for media struggling to engage their public with the EU: it will make it harder for reporters to attempt to explain the substantive decisions and policies under discussion in the Union. For a journalism which claims to hold power to account and act in the public interest, it is likely to do little. For a journalism which wants to interest the people, it is a large step forward.

2

The Limits of Utopia: Leaving Loyalty, Embracing Scepticism

> We are definitely a little bit less into utopia.
> (Philippe Ricard, *Le Monde*, Brussels correspondent)

At the beginnings of the European project, the press room in Brussels was mainly inhabited by believers in the European project. In the post-war period, a more plural UK press was divided, reflecting political parties' reluctance to join – but by the 1975 referendum, called to reject or endorse the UK's membership formalised three years earlier, the British press were largely in favour of 'yes' to membership of the EU.

There were French correspondents in Brussels by 1950, when the Agence France Presse (AFP) sent a correspondent to cover the High Authority in Luxembourg and then to Brussels – and, according to some, the French shaped the way the EU is still reported. Many correspondents were not professional journalists but rather young interns at the Commission who chose another career while remaining in the institution. 'The main characteristic of these young people [at the time]', says a report on coverage of the EU, 'was that they had no journalistic experience when they started to work for specialized media'.[1] They moulded Brussels reporting in their own way, fitting it 'with their own characteristics: technical knowledge and expertise, and an incredible address book that gives access to most officials'.[2]

This generation grew older, naturally, but their influence did not vanish entirely. 'They were known by everybody and were considered as the "great ancients", those who discovered and invented Brussels correspondence.'[3] The EU project was so complex that it needed interpreters rather than watchdogs at the time, and the EU correspondents were large personalities or were considered so within their newspapers.

The new organisation inspired loyalty. Two reasons are adduced for this attitude. First of all, the pioneer-correspondents felt the project was a leap in the dark, a wholly new form of organisation, neither a state like France nor an international institution like the United Nations – fragile, tentative, and best shielded from radical criticism.

Second, they were trying to give importance to their work and persuade editors to grant space to articles which by their subject matter and the uniqueness of the institution described were hard to simplify and hard to grasp: yet were still supportive. 'Between the 1950s and the 1990s there was a journalism here that was very militant. Journalists came here because they were very passionate about Europe and would never write anything against it – apart from the British, who were a class apart', according to Jean Quatremer (see Appendix 2) who has been writing for the French leftist newspaper *Libération* for the last 24 years. In his view, journalists were 'part of the project, they were not journalists, they were enthusiasts' and tended to make sure that 'everything negative was covered up'.

The influence of the men who were the architects of the Union was still, after all, strong: and the energy and idealism they brought to their mission, strongly marked as they were by the scarring experience of the Second World War, was an inspiration for a generation of journalists who had themselves experienced the war. There was a genuine feeling of being on the right side of history.

These figures included Konrad Adenauer, first Chancellor of the Federal Republic of Germany and in that post 1949–63, who saw reconciliation with France as his main foreign policy aim; the British wartime prime minister Winston Churchill, who called for a 'United States of Europe' to help eliminate more wars (but assumed that the UK, with its worldwide, still imperial, role would not be a part of it); Alcide De Gasperi, at different times Foreign Minister and Prime Minister of Italy, 1945–53, pressing for Italy to achieve 'normality' through close involvement in the European Union project; Walter Hallstein, the German legal academic who became the first, strongly federalist, President of the European Commission, 1958–67; Sicco Mansholt, the Dutch farmer and resistance fighter who set the basis for the Common Agricultural Policy; the French Jean Monnet, whose ideas on European integration were among the most influential in the late 1940s and 1950s, and which underpinned the plan – partly realised – to merge Europe's heavy industries; Robert Schuman, born in Alsace-Lorraine when it was a French possession but for a period after its annexation a German citizen, a politician (twice Prime Minister of France) who, with Monnet, devised the Schuman Plan for industrial integration; Paul-Henri Spaak, the Belgian politician in exile in London during the war, who, during the Messina conference in 1955, was charged with formulating the fundamentals of what became the Common Market; and Altiero Spinelli, perhaps the most enthusiastic of the pioneer federalists who, as a member of the Italian Communist Party in prison in 1941, wrote a manifesto 'For a free and United Europe', arguing that even if the fascist powers were defeated, a return to a Europe of Nations would inevitably lead to renewed war.

These men were deeply marked by the war through which they had, as mature adults, come: and were imbued with the common determination that it should be a war which *did* end all – at least European – wars. They were of a strongly tested generation: and their huge achievement in setting in place the foundations of what became the EU (along with the thousands more who worked along the lines they had set out) – coupled with the desire for peace in countries which had experienced horrors in wartime and desperate poverty and near starvation in the immediate post-war years – was their strongest argument.

But their vision, and the memories of war's horrors, and those of the war's aftermath, inevitably faded – even though the walls and corridors of the Commission building carry their photographs, busts, and sayings. The founders could not pass on their urgency for the completion of a unified Europe, nor even the moral force of its pacific mission. The EU, as an institution, became more ordinary, and thus moved within the scope of properly sceptical (as distinct from Eurosceptical), rather than reverential, journalism. This marked a shift in the representations of the EU which the journalists assigned to cover it think is significant: a change which is likely to be permanent, which has had and will continue to have deep effects on the way in which the Union and its institutions are perceived.

That a centre of political power should be treated as such – that is, in broadly the same ways in which national governments, parliaments, and political parties are treated: with (depending on the journalistic culture) usually little deference and an appetite for poking about in dark corners and ambiguous projects – demotes its institutions from being seen as instruments of peace, prosperity, and freedom. They became instead centres of high ideals, hard policy work, and ambitious programmes, but also of calculation, compromise, and manoeuvre: the necessary accoutrements of all politics. It was the most important transformation until the present economic crisis.

11

In the 1970s and 1980s, this sense of riding the wave of history started showing the first cracks. The post-war narrative lost part of its appeal. The signature of the Maastricht Treaty, in 1992, represented both an upgrade and a loss of innocence in the public's perception. In his memoir, the former high-ranking EU Commission official Riccardo Perissich says that the Treaty 'opened the doors to the popular emotions', while failing to 'create a political system able to convey them'. He reports a German official back in 1992 as saying: 'You have wanted more powers, and now you have to endure the consequences. Welcome to the club of scapegoats.'[4] At this time the first TV debates were held, dragging the EU into the 'field of democratic debate', which 'in the short history of the Community had never been seen before', according to Paul Collowald, former spokesperson of the Commission.[5]

While this institutional turning point was taking place, changes were under way in the press room as well. Quatremer says that 'something changed, in particular when in the 1990s Philippe Lemaître [the fiercely pro-European correspondent of *Le Monde*] left, and the Brussels news media world began to change': militants were replaced by people who had a different, less supportive approach towards the EU. This did not mean the end of journalism considered as an 'integrative performance',[6] that is, an activity aimed at accompanying and strengthening the EU political integration process. What happened was rather a change of perspective, largely due to an enlarged horizon and to a genuine increased curiosity. 'In the 1990s in France there was an infatuation both from the media and from the public for the EU topic', recalls Karl De Meyer, who was in Brussels for the French economic newspaper *Les Échos*. He mentions the positive impact that the German reunification, which happened rather smoothly, had on the French public, and the enthusiasm for the Eastern enlargement. 'The French had the feeling they were mending a historic mistake, having left the East to Soviets in 1945', he says.

The growing enthusiasm for the EU project increased the press coverage and opened the doors to a new generation of people with a conventional journalist background, some of whom applied the quotidian duty of journalism to investigate claims and policies more carefully than in the past, implicitly conceding that the institutions had sufficient strength to undergo their fair share of scrutiny and criticism.

One result of this change of attitude is that 'there is much more competition among journalists', according to Ruth Berschens, bureau chief of the German business daily, *Handelsblatt*. The generational clash was inevitable, with young journalists accusing the older ones of being too cosy with the Commission, while the latter blamed the young for their supposed ignorance. But the EU project was enjoying great momentum, and no one really criticised it in its entirety. There were new publications dedicated to the EU – *The European* funded by Robert Maxwell in 1990 and bought by the Barclay brothers in 1992 is a good example. Together with *Le Monde*, a French version was launched in 1998, with the idea of 'talking about the European way of life, the new emerging European society, also hard news', says De Meyer. 'There was a section called "European worksite" in which they weren't afraid of detailing the directives and regulation projects.' The French project failed after a few months, while the British edition lasted until 1998. But the interest was still relatively high, and many newspapers increased their presence in Brussels with a second correspondent.

An assignment to Brussels was usually good news for a journalist and at least for large newspapers the job came with the prestige of an almost ambassadorial status. As a major hub for decision-making, and as a crucial centre of power, the Belgian capital ranked among the more desirable assignments, not far below Washington and on a par with Beijing and Moscow. Unlike many other capitals, Brussels is a place where contacts are easy and where long-standing relations are built, in part thanks to the relatively small size of the city, where the EU area is enclosed within a particular district.

The quality of life in Brussels, both its advantages and its drawbacks, not only drew together the journalists, but their sources too: a grey and rainy city, Brussels has vast apartment blocks and a relatively inexpensive lifestyle, an interesting cultural life, a multilingual population with access to an international school, and a central position which allowed Brits, French, and Germans to settle down there without feeling too far from home. Not only did they live close to each other: journalists also worked in the same buildings, where their media organisation could rent an office. The Residence Palace, a beautiful art nouveau block once used as a Nazi headquarters, and the IPC, the International Press Centre, even closer to the Berlaymont building, still host the overwhelming majority of EU correspondents. Only the *Financial Times* has a separate bureau, facing the Palais Royal of Brussels and relatively distant from the EU citadel. 'The EU has grown enormously in the last 20 years – in the 1990s it was very small', maintains Ruth Berschens, saying that 'at the time it was maybe more like a family.' Outsiders would accuse them of being clubby. In many ways, they *were* clubby.

The Brits peeled off from the 'club' earlier than others. In the 1980s, as wartime memories faded, the UK press became emotionally more detached from the project. Dick Leonard, a correspondent for *The Economist* in the 1980s (his son, Mark Leonard, created and directs the pro-EU European Council for Foreign Relations), recalls 'a cosy relationship between the correspondents and the officials and commissioners' and says this was true, at that time, for British journalists as well.

In his view, the British journalists fitted, more or less, into an approach not so much friendly as collusive, a willingness to support the project by omitting its darker areas, fearing that surrounding enemies would profit from their revelations. Leonard found that even in the 1980s, the old habit of deference to the official position was still strong: and that it was bolstered by the capture of the journalists of different nationalities by their fellow nationals who were ministers and spokesmen and spokeswomen, and who fed journalists the lines most convenient to the governing powers, and to the European Union itself.

In 1989 Charles Grant – now head of the pro-EU think tank the Centre for European Reform – went to cover Europe for *The Economist*. Between his taking the post and Dick Leonard leaving it there was a four-year break: the then editor of the newspaper, Andrew Knight, thought the EU dull, and wanted to release funds for a Singapore bureau in the developing East. In Grant's view 'most of the Brits in the 1990s were pro-EU, though they did tend to stick with other Anglophones', while Lemaître, 'an important correspondent, something of a doyen', was very close to Jacques Delors and his cabinet when he took over in 1985. He was 'a bit pompous, very amenable to the line put out by the Commission', says Grant.

UK politics, up to the early 1980s, had seen the central ground of politics strongly supportive of the EU. In the 1980s, the Labour Party swung back from a radical socialist period to its usual left-of-centre position, and became an increasingly enthusiastic adherent of a Union which was, from 1985, supervised by Jacques Delors. A French Christian socialist, former MEP, and Cabinet Minister under François Mitterrand in the early 1980s, he made the inclusion of the Labour Party into the circle of Euro enthusiasts a particular, and successful, mission.

As Labour embraced the EU, the Conservative Party grew cold on it: the Margaret Thatcher-led Conservative government began to see the EU as an institution which not only took a disproportionate amount of UK contributions, but which also threatened and diluted the sovereignty of

Parliament. In 1988, in Bruges, she gave a landmark speech which took the name of the Belgian city in which it was given – and which was taken as a drawing of her red lines on what the UK would and would not countenance in the EU's development.

The 'guiding principle' was that 'to try to suppress nationhood and concentrate power at the centre of a European conglomerate would be highly damaging and would jeopardise the objectives we seek to achieve' and that 'we have not successfully rolled back the frontiers of the state in Britain, only to see them re-imposed at a European level with a European super-state exercising a new dominance from Brussels'.[7]

She and others, including, across the political divide, the leftist Labour former minister, the late Tony Benn, believed that Parliament was, and would and should remain, the focus of popular political loyalty and aspirations for political change. The language of Euroscepticism slowly became a passionate rhetoric of freedom, democratic accountability, and national values, while Europhiles relied on rationality, longer-term benefits, common rules, and the challenges of globalisation, which demanded large agglomerations of power.

The continental media continued to give great importance to their Brussels correspondents and the 'integrative performance' was maintained. 'In the 1990s Brussels correspondents were much more important within their respective papers compared to now: indeed, in Italy they approached the status of celebrities, among their readers. It is not the case any more', says Federico Fubini, who covers the European Central Bank and European Union from Italy for *La Repubblica* and who has long experience as a journalist in Brussels. The celebrity status could be due to the fact that journalists in Southern countries and in France were interpreters of the EU institutions, acting as guarantors and guardians of the obscure activities taking place in Brussels. They were the 'face' of the EU.

One of the most debated issues among reporters is whether experience is more important than having a fresh eye when it comes to covering the EU. The French AFP introduced a rotation system and journalists cannot stay more than five years. In Germany too they tend to change assignment after three or five years; the same is usually true of US and UK correspondents, though in the *Guardian* bureau both John Palmer in the past and Ian Traynor in the present are long-serving. French and Italian correspondents are also typically assigned for longer periods.

Another sign that the wind was changing between the 1980s and the 1990s is that the press campaigns targeting Brussels' institutions became more widespread. John Palmer, who covered the EU for most of a long career, and was based there from the 1970s to the 2000s, latterly as political director for the think tank the European Political Centre, says that 'the scepticism in the 1980s wasn't about the institutions or the EU itself', but it was rather 'about individual officials and their competence'. There 'were exposures of the abuse of funds' and of mismanagement, like the ones which led to the resignation of the entire commission headed by the Luxembourg-born Jacques Santer in 1999.

Libération's Jean Quatremer and the press in general played an important role in uncovering the scandal which famously involved the former French Prime Minister Edith Cresson who hired her dentist as an AIDS expert; there were also exposures of the activities of German, Spanish, and Portuguese members of the Commission. The French magazine *Le Nouvel Observateur* wrote at the time, 'whether it's good news or not, Europe, under the pressure of Northern protestant societies, entered a new era', one where 'public morality has higher requirements, which does not rule out hypocrisy'. According to the authors of the article, Cresson's mistake was to 'bring *Libération* to court for defamation', upsetting the media sector of the entire continent, and failing to understand that there was a 'new world emerging in Brussels'.[8]

Using the categories provided by Paolo Mancini and Daniel Hallin in their seminal study *Comparing Media Systems*,[9] it is clear that these three models of media systems met in Brussels and exercised some influence on each other. The Mediterranean or polarised pluralist model of France and Italy met and was, journalists from these countries claimed, substantially affected by the North Atlantic or liberal model of Britain and, naturally, also by the democratic corporatist model of Northern states like Germany. Hallin and Mancini believe that, since the 1970s, the differences have diminished and that in the space of one generation, media systems have been progressively, but not completely, homogenised along the lines of the liberal model.[10] Even though strong national differences remain and are clearly visible in Brussels, the influence of Anglo-Saxon investigative journalism has become embedded.

The ideological background, nevertheless, was untouched. Covering scandals was not an attack on the European ideal, and was not seen as such by most of the journalists who pursued these investigations: they were, however, seen by the older generation and by the spokespersons' service as being detrimental to the institutions and the fragile balance on which they relied. Quatremer still recalls that 'when I was doing a series of enquiries into the mad cow affair in the late 1990s, a colleague told me – "Stop, Jean, if you carry on like this you will sink the European project."'

The fear voiced then within the EU community was not that the institutions would be fundamentally challenged as being a political excrescence – as presently – but that challenges to the integrity of its officials would leech away trust in its actions. Euroscepticism was still quite a niche trend. According to Berschens, 'in the 1990s there were Eurosceptic journalists, but they were outside the mainstream, and Germans were not among them'. And even though criticisms could be very vocal, 'the scepticism about the project as a whole came much later', says Palmer.

A traditionally pro-European country like France changed its attitude towards the EU in the 2000s. The directive on the liberalisation of services in the EU internal market presented in 2004 by the Dutch Frits Bolkestein, a member of the Commission headed by the former Italian Prime Minister Romano Prodi, was perceived as the first step towards an economically liberal EU, bringing more disadvantages than advantages. It was the moment where the EU stopped being an extension of France – as French correspondents like to put it, the 'EU was a French idea paid for by Germans' – and became a foreign body, almost hostile. 'The years 2000 are the ones of the disconnection of France and Germany', says De Meyer, arguing that the EU was 'from that moment on perceived as an accelerator of a globalisation considered as nefarious, bringing more inequalities and making life harder for those with fewer qualifications'. This feeling was further reinforced by the EU enlargement and the arrival of new member states, often pro-American, and pro-free market. They ensured that the shift towards English as the official language, already begun with the arrival of the Scandinavian countries in the mid-1990s, became even more pronounced: the elites of the new entrants spoke English, not French.

This was the beginning of a new, more serious form of scepticism, one stemming from some loss of faith in the bigger project. The rejection of the EU Constitution project by French and Dutch voters in 2005 marked a low point, but the economy was still relatively buoyant and there was a feeling that problems could still be fixed over time. When the Lisbon Treaty – the text prepared to replace the ambitious project of an EU constitution – was signed in December 2007, the EU institutions were not so much under the spotlight. It was a relatively calm moment; the institutional reforms were so technical that the public did not show much interest, and when Lehman Brothers failed, American capitalism was the evil to blame and the EU a relatively peaceful haven.

The Greek debt crisis blew that away. Euroscepticism became more prevalent in countries where it was already a significant force, while in places like Italy or Greece, where pro-EU feelings were stronger in the past, the approach became closer to a sort of Euro-vandalism: the sudden and vocal desecration of something which was previously considered untouchable.

There were two main triggers for this change of attitude: the worsening economic conditions due to the euro-crisis and, as a consequence, an approach to immigration which saw liberal and conservative positions more obviously at war. The issue became 'very important, the most important at times' dividing public opinion, according to Hughes Beaudouin (see Appendix 3), the correspondent for the French TV channel LC1, part of TF1, the most popular channel in France with a share of about a quarter of the country's TV viewers. 'You have to remember that 20 years ago there was consensus on most subjects and there were fewer subjects. And now there isn't,' he says, describing the evolution of the EU as being 'much more political', since it 'concerns itself increasingly with stuff which is internal to the countries: and crucial to the battle between right and left'. Or, as some political observers have pointed out, the battle between populists and liberals, between 'ordinary people' and the elite. Because of the debt crisis, the preoccupations of ordinary people 'are more evident – and the system has become more open, more democratic', says Beaudouin. 'There's more confrontation because it's less administrative' than it used to be.

Beaudouin describes a system which had lost its innocence in the eyes of its closest observers. In becoming 'political' it has, as he says, become more open: but it has also entered into areas of political contention, and thus become less rarefied, more politically potent. This means that reporters could hardly treat EU politicians' actions with less scrutiny than they did governments and ministries in their home countries.

This shift required some revolutionary changes in economic management and in people's lives which were hard to accept both by 'weaker' countries, which felt they were living under the control of bigger states, and by wealthier countries like Finland and Germany, where the benefits of being part of the EU family are often upstaged by the fear they come at too high a cost. 'I think in Germany many voters feel betrayed – that they gave up the mark on the promise that other countries in the euro would be as disciplined financially as they – and now they are being blamed for not helping these countries who irresponsibly ran up debt which the Germans see as having been created by they themselves', says

Dirk Schuemer (see Appendix 5), an influential political columnist on Europe for the *Frankfurter Allgemeine Zeitung* (*FAZ*), whose strongly pro-integrationist stance has been questioned (by himself) in the last few years because of what he sees as the EU's inability to fulfil either its promise or its agenda. As a result, his columns are increasingly similar to the themes of the Eurosceptics.

As political correspondent in London for the same newspaper, Jochem Buchsteiner closely follows the British debate about the EU and is finding his readers increasingly interested in it. He confirms Germans' unquestioned support is now being interrogated, and at times wears thin. 'In Germany all the serious newspapers were very pro-European', says Buchsteiner, who used to work for *Die Zeit*. 'Now there is an eroding belief in the euro and things which would have not even being discussed before are now on the table'; he suggests that 'the aim of enlarging and deepening the Union at the same time was a contradiction which is becoming more and more obvious'. It is true, of course, that criticism was lively before, and many – not just the British sceptics – questioned almost everything the Commission and other institutions did. But there was a considerable difference: 'Everything was discussed even then, but this sense of a Great Goal is now lost', states Buchsteiner. Says Berschens: 'We became more sceptical because of what happened then – the unthinkable happened.'

Some demur. Philippe Ricard, until recently the correspondent for *Le Monde*, does not think the end of the 'utopian phase' of the EU is necessarily a bad thing for journalists: 'Jobs in Brussels', he says, 'have never lost their prestige; it is a great post'. And after the devastating recent debt crisis, he says, any dip in the importance of the post that might have occurred has been reversed. 'The job has become more exciting and less predictable.'

Being a correspondent in Brussels requires, or should ideally require, an uncommon set of skills, among which is the ability to cover a wide array of topics and fluency in more than one language. Language is not only a practical issue, but a very political one too. There was a time when governments would speak only to their national press. John Palmer, former European Editor of the *Guardian*, says that 'The big powers were very secretive; the French didn't allow any non-French journalists into their briefings.'

Palmer, however, determined to break this national exclusiveness: he, an Anglo-Saxon, inserted himself into a national briefing of President Valéry Giscard d'Estaing, and asked a question in French. In Palmer's recollection, Giscard told him that his accent was 'even further out than

Brittany'. Perhaps jolted out of its rut by Palmer's impudence, the system eventually began 'to break up' and it 'became obvious that you should open up the briefing to everyone,' says Dick Leonard. It was a matter of influence for bigger countries, and one of interest for journalists, as smaller countries' briefings were 'in general much more helpful, and they were more impartial about many of the issues. The different nationalities spoke to their national representations. The Irish representation was extremely indiscreet and would hand out confidential documents freely' – a press-friendly habit which would be picked up by the Central European latecomers.

French had been the lingua franca of the EU: English was used less, and German, the third official working language, was never widespread. Nevertheless, being fluent in several languages has always helped journalists in finding sources among the legion of diplomats, officials, and lobbyists handling EU affairs. Language is the key to open a whole set of national issues and points of view. Brussels is not so much a melting pot as a place where many national identities meet while keeping their character.

According to Paul Taylor, 'Europe had two heydays'. The first one was the signing of the Maastricht Treaty[11] in 1992. It came 'soon after the fall of the Berlin Wall' and was a 'time of great optimism and sense of a great future'. It brought some additional scrutiny and a whole new set of expectations to the project. The second was the 'eastward expansion after the end of communism in Central and Eastern Europe, which went on till the mid-2000s'.

Both events changed the way the EU was reported, bringing new journalistic cultures into the Brussels arena, and there were efforts to help new entrants to meet the EU journalistic standards. At the end of the Cold War in the late 1980s, the first strong attempts were being made to develop new visions, methods, and journalism training in the new European sense. One significant result had been the foundation of a transnational association of institutions of journalism. The EJTA (European Journalist Training Association) was created to 'conceptualize initial training models for a new type of European journalism' and led to the establishment of the European Journalism Centre (EJC) in 1993 in Maastricht. They provided 'introductory training courses for journalists from Central and Eastern European countries during the early years after the end of the Cold War, workshop series for regional journalism emphasizing European aspect'.[12] On and off, the EJC has acted as a 'partner institution of the EU

Commission, and still operates within a framework contract on the basis to provide journalism training for reporting Europe'. Suspicion that it prepares journalists not just to report, but to report positively on the EU is reasonable: no other journalism school in a democratic state is a 'partner institution' of a government, or a legislature.

The number of accredited journalists in the EU press room reflected these changes. After the collapse of the Soviet bloc, Brussels started hosting more reporters than any other institution in the world, including the White House. The Commission, understandably, was very proud of this evolution. Germans were always the largest group, even though their number slightly declined from 138 in 2002 to 126 in 2013.

Says John Palmer, 'There had been a very large British press corps – the *Guardian* had 3–4 people; *Times* 2–3; *FT* 5 or 6; and the BBC had 30–40 people'.[13] Even the tabloids, at the time, had correspondents: 'The *Mirror* had 1–2 correspondents, the *Daily Express* had 1, the *Mail* had 1. Then they disappeared'. Figures from the Commission show the UK media had 95 accredited people in 2002 and 118 in 2013, that Spain went from 63 to 72, with 42 media registered. France went from 55 to 60 in little more than a decade, but the number of media grew from 26 to 42. Greece, according to figures, remained almost stable, while the Italian corps went from 44 to 65 members. Official figures for accredited journalists in 2002 were 878, reached 1,031 in 2005, and then remained just below the 1,000 threshold for some years. In 2013 accreditations reached the historic peak of 1,095. Among them 406 are women, compared to 275 in 2002.

Thus when everyone talks about a decline in the presence of the press in Brussels, figures show the exact opposite. The answer to this apparent contradiction has to do with the evolution of journalism itself: in 2003 there were only two freelancers, in 2013 there were 54. Those figures probably substantially underestimate the reality, because many freelancers actually get an accreditation with one of the many media outlets to which they contribute on a freelance basis, as it is much harder to obtain access to the EU institutions as an independent. In Brussels, as elsewhere, there is a strong hierarchy among journalists in access to sources.

Journalistic presence has not declined in terms of numbers: on the contrary. But it has become more precarious, more fragmented, with people who have to work under an additional pressure – financial and practical – compared to earlier correspondents. The overall number of media organisations accredited went from 574 in 2002 to 624 in 2003. Their number then stabilised, and declined to the current 557 in 2013.

There are many levels of EU journalism, and many media entirely dedicated to the EU: *EU Observer*, EurActiv.com, MyEurop, EUBusiness, Presseurop, Eurotopics, Café Babel, *Euros du village* (*The Euros*), *Le Taurillon* (*The New Federalist*), Agence Europe, Europolitique, *European Voice*, *New Europe*, *Parliament Magazine*, *EU Reporter* and E!Sharp. The often detailed coverage of these outlets is much amplified by the publications of think tanks, law firms, and lobbyists. There are the big agencies – Reuters, Bloomberg, Dow Jones, AP, and AFP – which pump out a great deal of material from relatively well-staffed bureaux, and there is the plethora of specialist media, covering everything from agriculture to antitrust in a detailed way for their professional readership. On technical, specific issues, there was seldom space for scepticism, and the specialist press has always been blessed by having a committed readership, often small, but one whose interest could be taken for granted.

The 'utopia' which is part of the title of this chapter is used with some irony, but also literally: Thomas More's *Utopia* assumed an orderly society in which everyone agreed on its goodness and order – as, according to the testimonies of past and present correspondents, the early reporters and early officials largely did of the early Union. The contemporary mores of journalism, commonly thought of as Anglo-Saxon in inspiration, don't tolerate such identity of view between describers and described: thus the journalism of the EU has, in the main, conformed with that elsewhere in free societies.

3

Communicating to the Communicators: How the EU Presents Itself

> The EU has an interest in surviving, just like any other bureaucratic system.
>
> (Matina Stevis, *Dow Jones-Wall Street Journal*)

Every day at midday Brussels correspondents gather in the press room of the EU Commission to attend the briefing. As they file in, they glance at the press releases on display at the entrance, looking for relevant decisions which have to be communicated immediately by real-time media like newswires, radio, TV, internet. The press releases are written in a succinct and technical style, with a quote from the competent commissioner announcing that the news is good, the particular initiative is worthwhile and much needed, the revealed problem resolved or being tackled, the transgression by country A over regulation Z being dealt with.

There are often a dozen or more of them, particularly on Wednesdays, when the Commission meets and infringement procedures are launched against member states who have not applied the EU law, or closed when governments comply. These press releases, carefully prepared, are the small bricks on which the EU information is built. They are a way to feed journalists with enough news to keep them busy, at least for a couple of hours. The briefing starts: the news of the day is presented and questions are taken, sometimes answered, sometimes stonewalled. The whole thing lasts up to one hour, and is always attended by several dozen journalists, while others watch it via streaming video from their offices. Often it is preceded or followed by a technical briefing held off the record by officials in order to provide background information on a regulation or a directive, or by a press conference by one of the commissioners.

At the end of the briefing journalists gather around a spokesperson and ask additional questions, to which the answers are off the record. This exercise can take up to half an hour and tends to be more useful than the briefing itself, because the questioning concerns a particular topic and is less formal than the one taking place in the press room. The spokespeople often claim that it is the only institution on earth which invites journalists to ask any question, every day. It is certainly the case that the noon conference is an open forum; however, it's not true that it's unique. Many parliaments and governments brief political correspondents at least once a day and the questions can range widely.

The first press service of what became the European Union was organised as soon as the institutions were established. It functioned, and was designed to function, as much to propagandise for Europe as to provide an information service about it. 'The spokesmen were good; they rarely tried to cover things up' and 'the head of the spokesman service was very influential', Dick Leonard says, adding that 'the French influence was dominant when I was there – Roy Jenkins when President appointed a Brit as spokesman and he was frozen out by the French.'

The general rule is that every commissioner should appoint a spokesperson from a different country than his own, but there are many exceptions to it, and the Brussels population is so international that there are many cases of people with three native languages and a double passport acting as spokespersons. The briefing takes place in French and English and the ability to switch from one language to the other is striking. National quotas in the spokesperson's service are unofficially yet widely applied, as was already the case in Leonard's times. 'It meant that the best person for the job often didn't get it.'

The communication decisions made by the spokespersons' meeting every morning at 10 for the midday briefing 'are spread all over Europe and the rest of the world' thanks to online streaming and 'that makes the process going on in Brussels all the more centralised in terms of what is diffused, irrespective of how it is diffused,'[1] writes Olivier Baisnée, a professor of political sciences in Toulouse, author of several studies on the EU and the press.

Most correspondents interviewed had a more downbeat view of the service provided by the spokespeople – even as they all reckon that the spokespersons service hosts many people who are expert in the field they cover. The service was thoroughly reformed by the former President of the EU Commission, Romano Prodi, who in the aftermath of the resignation of the Cresson scandal tried to change the approach to communication in order to have a stronger grip on the press room and avoid competition among spokespersons, which could lead to scandals and leaks. Prodi famously contacted Alastair Campbell, who at the time was Tony Blair's spin doctor, and the BBC for advice,[2] and in a speech at the EU Parliament in Strasbourg in September 1999 he spoke about a new 'glasnost', or in his version transparency, which had to rule the EU activities under his presidency. The strategy adopted included an attempt to focus the news media's attention on one piece of news per day: but without success. The reason is simple: 'While it is possible to predict the wishes of a national press it becomes much harder when there are 15 national presses with as many specific priorities and agendas.'[3]

In our interviews, there did not seem to be a single journalist in Brussels willing to give unqualified praise to the midday briefing. 'Nothing much is said,' says the *FT*'s Peter Spiegel, who uses the daily appointment 'mostly for socialising'. Quatremer is blunt, considering the press service 'useless' and points out that before Prodi it was 'different, you could eat with them, talk to them', while now spokespersons 'are shut in their offices' and they see the media 'as enemies'. Matthias Krupa of *Die Zeit* maintains he is 'still astonished' by the press service. 'On the one hand there is much more help', he says, mentioning the 'way they explain the technical issues – much better than in Germany'. On the other hand, 'they give you the information they want to give' and 'if you have a question they don't want to answer, or a question which doesn't fit into the scheme they find it much more difficult'.

A revealing note sent to the spokespersons of each of the 20 commissioners helps us understand the mentality of both the commissioners and the press spokespersons in the late 1990s. Martine Reicherts was then the head of communications, one who had to manage more scandals than anyone else in her position to date. 'There certainly is an uptake of the press room by investigative journalists, yet it is wrong to say that we don't have friends any more', she wrote in January 1999, just a couple of months before the Santer team resignation. She pointed out that 'on the contrary' some journalists disapprove 'sometimes openly of the outrageousness of their colleagues'. The spokespersons' strategy will therefore be 'to use potential allies to bring back a balance between investigative journalists and background journalists', taking into account that 'a certain dose of cynicism – and sometimes of hypocrisy – in the way we spread information is sometimes necessary'.

In Reicherts's view, given that some journalists are 'particularly twisted', spokespersons have to force themselves to 'freeze part of the information', because 'over-information often borders with disinformation'.[4] Prodi's reform, according to several journalists, took this approach to the next level.

However, the tornado triggered by the debt crisis that began in 2009–10 led the Commission to react promptly by appointing Koen Doens, a former Belgian diplomat, Flemish, head of the spokesman service. 'Better – very sympathetic', says Quatremer. The arrival of Doens was welcomed by most of the press room, perceived as he is as less of a Eurocrat than others. 'He never appears but he does speak off the record; and he's good, he speaks about the politics behind the norm', according to Peter Spiegel, who says it is 'still very hard to get anything out of the Commission – you have to go to the different countries'. Spiegel agrees on Doens: 'he's different – he's not a creature of the EU ... he has a different view of the world. He doesn't think everyone who is here from the press is a national champion.'

Reicherts's note in 1999 clearly reveals her nostalgia for the time when communicators and journalists had a cosier relationship, in large part because of the unchallenged role then played by the European Commission. 'The influence of the Commission has waned. Nationalism has gained ground – and with it a more aggressive style of press– Commission relations', says Dick Leonard, who recalls that in the 1980s and 1990s 'the midday press conference was the main source of stories for most correspondents'.

French was the official language and the press conferences were given in French without any translation. 'Still, the great majority of the questions were asked by the British – in bad French', Leonard says. Thirty years on, some – all Brits – believe the British press corps contributes in creating a more competitive atmosphere during the briefings. Chris Morris of the BBC says that 'the thing that would be missing if the UK were to leave is that the Brits correspondents do ask the big questions. They always say – why are we doing things like that?'

Any exercise in public relations is naturally aimed at creating legitimacy, and much of the legitimacy and prominence of the Commission was due to its firepower in communication. During the debt crisis, part of its prestige was lost to other emerging communicators, such as the government in Berlin, but also the EU Council. *Gazeta Wyborcza* correspondent Tomasz Bielecki joins the majority when he says that 'the official communication is not very helpful, to be honest', because 'the Ecofin [Economic and Finance Committee, uniting the economic and finance ministers of the member states] and the [European] Council [of

Prime Ministers and Presidents] were much better in organising briefings and press conferences'.

Particularly useful are background off-the-record briefings, which have always been the EU Commission's speciality. But again, those held by the EU Council were '300% better than the ones from the Commission in explaining things in the background', according to the Polish journalist.[5] The evident 'feeling of intra-institutional competition' weakens the final result when it comes to the Commission. 'One of the reasons is that in fact they do not have anything to communicate; the most important comes from the other part of the street.'

'The EU has an interest in surviving, just like any other bureaucratic system', says Matina Stevis, a correspondent for *Dow Jones-Wall Street Journal*. She does not think the Commission has been 'responsible for anything' during the crisis, because they have been 'the weakest link' in the decision-making process and they get a lot of criticism just because 'they have staff' and are there to answer questions every day, getting much of the frustration. 'If anything, I think they get too much blame', she points out, noting that she seldom uses the midday briefing in building her stories.

As the crisis developed, the Commission's communication effort, however it was viewed, could not be ignored. 'Two years ago whatever they said was a market mover, really, but it is not the case any more, so we use it only when it is newsworthy', says Stevis. This considerably changed the attitude of the Commission, making it even more careful in the messages it was delivering: but care in delivery and confining oneself to the bare facts rarely wins plaudits from reporters.

Those who work for the various European institutions have a particularly delicate task: they are expected to be open and full in the information they give, but often walk on eggshells in giving it, because of the close scrutiny of national governments. This was especially the case at the peak of the financial crisis, since every word was highly market sensitive. Plus, member states are themselves easily moved to anger if a comment clashes with their own narratives about their economies and the measures being taken to mend them.

The issue is, once again, the battle to raise interest among the public when it comes to the 'on the record' communication. Tomasz Bielecki of *Gazeta Wyborcza* compares the information service in Brussels to that in Moscow, where he was earlier a correspondent – and speaks of the transition as from a famine to a feast. The downside, he says, is that when he was reporting from Russia, it was easier to persuade editors to publish a story: 'Anything about alcohol is easier to sell compared to the ECB and the spread [of interest rates].' The EU Commission does not manage to make its stories interesting, and according to most reporters, it is very hard to get rid of the pre-packaged taste many of them have.

Spokespersons of the Commission, just like any other PR representatives, also play a more informal yet crucial role in spinning news. The friendly relations they have with many journalists in the press room gives them some influence. Many members of the spokespersons' service were recruited from journalists and quite often their career did not stop on the podium of the press room: they became chef de cabinets, or held other roles within the Commission. Some spokespersons then went to work for PR firms – or even created them, in the case of Nigel Gardner, a former BBC journalist who worked as a spokesman for trade in the Commission and for the Labour group in the EU Parliament before co-founding GPlus, a successful communication strategy and political advocacy group.

The role of both communicators and journalists changed as Brussels became home to an increasing number of lobbyists and PR representatives, whose presence played an important role in providing journalists with alternative sources of information. George Candon, based in Brussels, working for the consulting and public relations company FTI, says that 'there's been a much greater professionalisation of PR: we're being taken more seriously'. In his view 'a lot of shifts are happening: there used to be a pyramid of influencers – that's gone. The journalists were the gatekeepers – now they're part of a wider ecology.'

That 'wider ecology' is one made up of information, analysis, and comment: from agriculture to telecommunications, all those who need information related to their sector can easily find it. Journalism is bit by bit losing the privilege of determining what is more and what less significant. It is becoming, with some pain, part of a communications field in which different voices vie for supremacy, mainly on the internet. The high walls which separated it from amateur stabs at journalism on the one hand and the academy and learned professions on the other are falling away, just as one massive news media institution after another now abandons the grand citadels once built to contain their industrial might and shuffles off to a floor or two in anonymous office blocks.

Candon reflects the common view in contemporary PR: that is, that, as the professor of networking and former PR company head Julia Hobsbawm puts it, 'public relations may be suited to the manipulated and the hyperbolic, but it is also just as much about the truth as it is about anything else'.[6]

That view of their job is strongly held by the Brussels public relations staff. Once the correspondents adopted scepticism as their attitudinal stock in trade, they found themselves in conflict with a PR corps which insists on relaying what some of them see as a propagandist line. The newly sceptical attitudes carry with them – in nearly every context – an aggressive attitude to public relations (the attitudes will vary when public relations organise events to provide coverage). In the context of the EU, that has inevitably meant a relationship which is combative, and which can lead to mutual disappointment. Good journalism in Brussels is often defined by the distance taken from EU communication, which constantly promotes a strongly normative line on the EU in the face of the gathering distrust shown not only by some correspondents, but also by a large share of the public.

Unsurprisingly, then, a frequent journalists' complaint is that the service remains defensive, upset by negative stories, prone to asking journalists who write them why they are aiding the anti-EU enemies. 'You still see elements of the past, people who get grumpy about negative stories,' says Peter Spiegel, who believes that the EU risks being made weaker, not stronger, by an overprotective stance. The PR teams are good at communicating the benefits of the EU, he thinks, but the last few years have changed the situation: the EU is now a highly contested organisation, and mere assertion of its goodness will do little for it. 'There will be a debate, what's bad with the opposition?' he says. Krupa agrees that 'they are much more sensitive to criticism' since the crisis began. 'I feel like saying – we are media, you are politicians.'

But belief in the trustworthiness of the EU institutions, once considered a given, has declined in recent years. Many journalists say that, during the debt crisis, the Commission did not have the latest information, and thus was not the centre of power and of decision-making. On occasions, journalists were misled: the most famed case was that of a secret meeting which took place in May 2011 on a Saturday in Luxembourg. The spokesperson of the then President of the Eurogroup, now President of the Commission, Jean-Claude Juncker, repeatedly denied to the *WSJ* journalist Charles Forelle the fact of the secret summit, timed to take place at the peak of the Greek crisis. Juncker – who once famously said that 'When it becomes serious, you have to lie' – even followed the same line with the reporters who went to Luxembourg to doorstep, notwithstanding the denials. This episode was mentioned by many correspondents as the moment when the trust relation was broken. Yet many lies, or at least silences, were visited on the press by the leading actors in stemming the panic of prospective euro collapse: a sustained and illuminating three-part investigation by Spiegel in the *FT* in May 2014 showed, among much else, the large number of secret meetings, strategy developments, rows, deals, and betrayals which saving the euro – if it has been saved – seemed to demand.

The tendency to regard the EU communications function as at best unhelpful now seems rooted in most correspondents from most countries. Bernardo de Miguel from Spain's *Cinco Dias* says that 'the communication from the Commission has been simply awful' during the crisis, because 'they have missed everything, they have been always reacting late' and they did not manage to secure a space in an increasingly complex political arena. 'They try to do politics, but they are not able to', according to de Miguel, who thinks the 'Commission has been bypassed and everything now is intergovernmental'. In his view the perception of a democratic deficit in the Commission's role, 'the fact that they don't win elections', weakened it and made its message less authoritative. As a result, now it is more often seen as special pleading, or partial truth, or more simply irrelevant to the task in hand – which, for the journalists, is to cover a vast financial crisis.

To frame the issue as a battle between the journalists and the public relations staff is only part of the story. As important – at times more important – is the battle, hidden from view, between two classes of political communicators – the EU staff and the staff of the visiting ministers, especially prime ministers on their visits to Council of Europe meetings. Nick Robinson, the BBC's political editor, who accompanies the UK Prime Minister to EU summits (but has never worked in Brussels) told a seminar in October 2013 at King's College London that there is a set of stories for a UK reporter at the summits: the 'wicked Eurocrats' story; 'Britain isolated' story; and the 'PM defies Brussels' story, a pattern most often used, he said, by former Prime Minister Gordon Brown.

This kind of spin is particularly effective for several reasons. The first one, according to Robinson, is that people who come in and out in a day or two do not have Brussels contacts, and therefore they rely on national backgrounders. When a summit is finished, there isn't much time to write a summary and the battle of communication is won by those who give the most succinct and most effective message. Analysis comes later and does not get as much attention. In Brussels, Chris Morris says that 'of course with the Westminster correspondents there's a bubble and it's cosy – it's just what happens'. The correspondents felt that they were victims of various streams of public relations – from national politicians at home, from leading politicians' PR people in Brussels, and from the Brussels communicators. All had a story to tell: often, these stories were different, sometimes starkly so.

To explain the difference existing among stories published in different countries, the European Editor of *The Economist*, John Peet, also speaking at the King's College seminar, points out that 'there is a tendency in every country to think that what is national is good and what comes from Brussels is bad'. The solution to this, according to Peet, is to widen the range of news reported and not issue them only from the EU institutions. 'Reporters in Brussels should try to get their stories from other EU capitals,' he says.

But when it comes to covering the EU, most Brussels correspondents can be said to resent a lack of resources: and their demands of the press service are frequently for rapid explanations across a range of issues which they can cover and thus understand only shallowly. This is frustrating for both sides: on the correspondents' side, an impatience to get at the meat of a story whose detail can often prevent them from grasping the essential element which would make a readable, or a televisual, story. On the communicators' side, there is a realisation that their expertise in a subject is largely wasted on their interlocutors in the news media.

Matthias Krupa of *Die Zeit* illustrates the problem by a comparison – 'the difference is that *Die Zeit* has some 15 correspondents covering German politics', while he is alone in Brussels. The national spin will easily prevail, in such a condition, since the EU is 'much more complex because of the numbers of institutions, the 28 countries, the divisions of power'. The fact that a correspondent 'can only give an idea, nothing like the full picture', helps us to understand why the EU Commission, at the time when it was still able to provide a reliable synthesis of a complex process, was the dominant source among journalists.

For Anton La Guardia of *The Economist*, whose main output has been until very recently the weekly Charlemagne column which rounds off the European section of his newspaper, the press service is, as one would expect, of variable quality, and no more – 'it depends very much on the person – some are very useful, some useless'. Correspondents do not lament the lack of availability of spokespersons, but their usefulness. 'I use them to check a fact. Some of them really are experts who know the details better than the officials', he reckons. For Hughes Beaudouin of France's

LC1/TF1, the problem is less obfuscation, rather fear to speak on the record, which is particularly problematic for a TV journalist. 'The officials tell us very interesting things but won't repeat it on the record', he says.

Matthias Krupa agrees that anonymous sources – 'a high-ranking official' or a 'European diplomat' – give a sense of secrecy which does not help the EU to be reported in a vibrant way. According to Beaudouin this is 'changing a bit', thanks to Olivier Bailly, the spokesman who usually gives the midday press briefing and who 'does play the role of spin doctor well. He is particularly concerned with France – he knows the political system very well – and how the media function.' He is influential among diplomats and politicians, 'he prepares himself well and identifies the important and touchy subjects', says Beaudouin, adding: 'He is an exception, a new experience for us.'

The EU's communicators are, as some of the journalists we interviewed attest, extremely sensitive about what is and what is not on the record. Much of this is due to the particular circumstances of their work. Where a spokesperson for a national leader has a certain degree of freedom in interpreting his principal's actions, a Commission spokesman is constantly reminded of how many people are finely tuned to the nuances of announcements made, and are easily roused to protest if they feel a briefing has been angled against their interests, national, political, or personal.

The inhibitions which this imposes upon the press service are considerable, and tend to enforce a style which cleaves tightly to the facts, to off- rather than on-the-record briefings and to European decisions which bind the member states. 'To be able to be on the podium, speaking in different languages, with an eye on what is going on around, being observed by the president, by the cabinet, by the commissioner, by the markets, by the press: don't make the mistake to underestimate them', says a European press spokesman.

Communicating the European Union is not something that happens only in Brussels: a great deal is done on a national level, bypassing the EU capital. In every member state there is one or more representation of the EU Commission, with an official or officials specifically assigned to communicate to media. The sensitivity about 'on the record' statements to the press extends to speaking about journalists (rather than to them): no member of the service whom we contacted would agree to be interviewed about those they work with on the record. The comments here are those of three experienced officials who presently deal or have dealt with the news media – call them PR1, PR2, and PR3.

First, there is the inherent difficulty, the source of much frustration in the relationship: the mismatch between detail and complexity on the one hand and the need to simplify with a strong uncluttered storyline on the other. In member states the difficulty is higher. Says PR1 (who works in a Southern country with a traditional pro-EU approach): 'The main difference is that Brussels is very auto-referential and you can rely on a shared knowledge which is much deeper than anywhere else even among media.'

Having to deal with a public opinion which is much more hostile to the EU, PR2 points out that 'European policy is hard to explain' and 'the process of reaching it is slow and tortuous, though it does involve ministers and parliaments of the member countries'. She complains that, in their quest for a wider readership, 'the press has dumbed down', pointing out how difficult it is to underline that the EU does not act through a 'diktat from Brussels' but thanks to decisions that need to 'be translated into national legislation'.

Details are lost, except in the specialised media, and the quality of what is published in the popular press is even worst than in the past. 'Even 25 years ago the tabloids would carry details of what was happening: now it's all polemic', PR2 points out, adding that 'that which is written is written back in the editorial offices and not reported from Brussels'. The BBC presence in the EU capital is not sufficient to counterbalance the far-reaching influence of tabloids, which 'affects the broadsheets as well in some measure'.

PR2 admits some responsibility for the overcomplexity: she says that, 'while it's true that complexity isn't avoidable, we can do more to make the material relevant', for instance on issues which can engage the public, like gardening. One vast problem is education on EU matters, which is weak everywhere. 'European literacy is weak, in particular when people do not know much about their own institutions', says PR1. 'The audiences to which the news media address themselves will themselves be resistant to detail, since they don't have the big picture', says PR2.

Being in the 'last outpost of the EU in member states' gives you a privileged point of view to understand what is going on at a national level. 'In Brussels criticisms are perceived, but I am not sure they are understood', because the headquarters 'have a difficulty in elaborating a coherent message which is translatable not only in different languages, but into different realities as well'.

Asked about the peculiar situation of the UK press, PR3 stresses the paradox of tabloid journalists who believe they 'hold the EU to account' and therefore feel justified for what they write. He believes that the question that needs to be asked is 'Do you hold the EU to account or do you give people the facts by which they could hold the EU to account themselves?' But it is useless to spend time 'fighting with the *Sun* and the *Mail*, even though people think it is what I do', because 'the tabloids' stance on the EU would not change because of EU communication' since it is 'made by editors, not by reporters'.

The strategy has to be proactive, and not too defensive. 'All you can do is try to get some good stories and say that something is not true when it is not true', he says. 'Our job is to make sure the information is factually correct, not to fight Euroscepticism. At least if they quote me saying that something is incorrect, that's something', he says.

Outposts of the EU Commission in member states are crucial to bring an informed opinion about those countries' evolutions. PR3 thinks the influence of tabloids is overestimated – 'it is a mistake to think that readers always believe what they read, and very often they buy the *Daily Mail* or the *Sun* to read about sports, not politics' – even though it is true that, compared to other member states' accession to the EU, 'the UK shuffled in reluctantly: it had a parliamentary structure at the core of its politics which goes back centuries and a recent imperial greatness'.

This is a hard fact, just like the fact that Europeans are much more interconnected than they were 20 years ago, even though, according to PR2, there 'was not the degree of aggression and confrontation there is today'. All of the anonymous PR executives say that, if the Commission did withhold some information at the peak of the crisis, it was for a good reason, which has not been explained enough. 'Otherwise', says one, 'Athens would have gone bust in a day'.

4

Growing Apart: The Argument over Objectivity

> In Brussels there is a tension between two jobs: reporting institutions as they are and the permanent debate about their legitimacy.
>
> (Nick Robinson, Political Editor of the BBC)

The liberal form of journalism, for those who attempt to do it properly, requires an attitude of professional and universal scepticism: that is, treating all information beyond the most obviously uncontestable as requiring some interrogation before being accepted. Normally, this does not extend to the need to question the existence of a constituted democratic body. Journalistic scepticism, especially about political power, coexists easily with acceptance of the given individual's or institution's right to exercise power where there is an explicit or implicit recognition that the sources of power, and the mechanisms by which it was achieved, have been democratically and civically tested and found sound.

Euroscepticism is not of that order: in the form it has taken for some years in the UK, and which has more recently become potent (in quite widely differing forms) in the Netherlands, in France, in Greece, in Finland, in Italy, and to a more limited degree in Germany – as well as in the Central and East European states which came into the EU in the early 1990s – Euroscepticism takes the position that the euro currency, and often the Union itself, are burdens on the nation state and on the national economies, and must be sloughed off. On which level does the 'impartial' journalist have to locate himself, from which assumptions does s/he have to report?

Bruno Waterfield (see Appendix 1), the *Daily Telegraph* correspondent in Brussels, is probably the most uncompromising Eurosceptic reporter for a mainstream news organisation in Brussels. His reports usually take a critical angle on the EU and on the legitimacy of its actions. In his view, the rest of the press is very 'clubby' and 'there is always a temptation to identify too closely with the project'. For every nationality there is 'a different way of dealing with that'.

Many of the journalists interviewed say objectivity is an illusion when it comes to the EU and that it is hard not to have your own opinions influence your work, because those opinions concern the very existence of the institutions you are reporting about. It is common to have Brussels correspondents for the continental press write abrasive articles about the EU, as critical as Eurosceptics. The difference is in the assumptions and in the conclusions: Europhiles call for changes but are deeply aware of how complicated they would be; Eurosceptics consider that the whole structure is, or should be, doomed.

Correspondents from most EU countries had, until the mid-2000s, worked within a framework of assumed public support 'back home' for the institution on which they were reporting. No longer. As Mark Leonard of the European Council for Foreign Relations wrote in April 2013, 'Euroscepticism has now spread across the continent like a virus.'[1] Echoing long-established Eurosceptic tropes, he adds that 'To an increasing number of citizens in Southern European countries, the EU looks like the IMF did in Latin America: a golden straitjacket that is strangling the space for national politics and emptying their national democracies of content.' On the other hand, in Northern European countries, 'the EU is increasingly seen to have failed as a controller for the policies of the southern rim'.

On both sides there is an increasing 'sense of victimhood' and 'if sovereignty is understood as the capacity of the people to decide what they want for their country, few in either the North or the South today feel that they are sovereign'. The general perception is that 'a substantial part of democracy has vanished at the national level but it has not been recreated at the European level'. The impact of the EU on citizens' lives has been so intrusive in the years of the financial crisis that it has been hard to make clear that the EU is made up of its member states and that its decisions are the outcome of long negotiations – that it is not an alien entity imposed from above.

This new (to many countries and journalists) public disillusionment, including from leading commentators who are strongly for greater unity in the EU such as Mark Leonard, has created an additional challenge for journalists, who can be tempted to pose as political actors either for or against the EU. The blame-game politicians played with Brussels to impose drastic financial cuts backfired; now, showing their independence from the EU institutions has become a crucial part of their political communications. Some journalists believe it is part of their job to defend Brussels from the accusations it gets every day.

Says Giovanna Pancheri of Sky Italia, an all-news channel, 'you cannot be objective about the EU', because 'it is inevitable that you have some preferences and choices'. Journalists 'don't have to show' those preferences, but 'Europe is the perfect scapegoat' and this, in her view, has to be made clear to viewers. 'Am I a Europhile? If you want to tell the story well, I think you become a little bit Europhile'. In her view the crisis increased the degree of integration among member states, but it led also to some questionable decisions, like imposing austerity measures on ailing economies. 'You become very critical, but my belief is pro-European,' she says, showing how pro-European attitude has changed over time.

Italy is a country with a very strong pro-EU history, though, as this is written, with a strong counter-movement against the EU for the first time. To work to further integration on any level has always been considered very prestigious – a view which has included journalists and which remains, for the majority, an all-but-unquestioned attitude, as it has for the majority in Germany. Many Italian reporters, more than those from any other major state, remain less convinced of the virtues of neutrality than others. They believe in the project, and think they should display their beliefs, which stems from a very argumentative media tradition.

They have a strong basis within their own profession and culture for this: the two most powerful figures in post-war Italian journalism, Eugenio Scalfari, founder of *La Repubblica* on the centre left, and Indro Montanelli, founder of *Il Giornale* on the liberal right, both believed that objectivity was not relevant to the journalism they practised, and the newspapers they created and edited. Both thought, instead, that journalism should be militant; that it should take a strong ideological position, be clear about it and promote it. Objectivity was not just unobtainable: it was irrelevant – worse, it was dishonest. Scalfari dismissed any efforts to be fair, balanced, neutral, or objective, scorning 'an illusory political neutrality' in favour of a journalism which was clearly engaged, which had 'explicitly chosen a side'. He was, he wrote, moving journalism from 'the passive to the active voice'.[2]

Enrico Tibuzzi, bureau chief of the ANSA press agency, respects the conventional 'Anglo-Saxon' bias towards having no bias, but in the end remains with Montanelli and Scalfari – 'the dynamics behind the press agencies are not always easy. Objectivity is always very relative. It is hard to reach because you have two different fronts, a personal and a professional, and personal beliefs matter, in the end.' His explanation of the 'respect' Italian public opinion used to have towards the EU is that 'it helped the country obtain reforms and benefits that otherwise no government would have had the guts to pass'. This is why 'it is a matter of honesty to say we are pro-European', since 'everyone has a background, it is useless to deny it'.

Federico Fubini of *La Repubblica* brusquely assumes the same position – 'neutrality is an illusion, but I try not to be influenced by my personal opinion'. To that, the adherents of the view that at least an effort to achieve objectivity is required would answer: everyone has opinions, but the journalistic responsibility in those services which proclaim, explicitly or implicitly, their neutrality is to strive for objectivity.[3]

A more insidious enemy of objectivity than personal bias is the hold which a particular narrative has over groups of journalists who – belying the competition which differing news organisations are supposed to maintain towards each other – cluster round one general interpretation in order not to be perceived, by their fellows and more importantly their editors, as eccentric. Andrew Gardner of the *European Voice* – one of the most diligent observers of the EU, written for the 'village' – says that 'a particular narrative can take hold and alternative narratives cannot gain ground and space due to structural issues, such as lack of staff'. In his view it is very hard to say whether a choice was made 'by default or for structural issues'.

The solution he has chosen to cover issues which are complex is to promote a debate on topics like banking union instead of hiding behind 'empty and dangerous phrases' like 'More Europe', which, he believes, reflect a dogmatic approach likely to backfire eventually. 'Having an open debate would not be helped if we were to stay in the trenches' for or against a topic. Plus, for *European Voice* 'the basic consensus is that what goes on in Brussels matters' and the 'tone of the analysis is to hold the EU institutions accountable'.

Matthias Krupa of *Die Zeit* puts the case for the demands of objectivity over the pull of personal opinion most clearly – 'I came here and still have a European-integration-friendly personal view; but my understanding as a journalist is not to fight for something, but to report', he says, pointing out that his 'friendly' approach is 'in accord with the view of *Die Zeit*'. In Germany, he claims, Euroscepticism does not exist as such, but there is a debate on 'how to save the euro', with pro- and anti-austerity fronts. 'And the mainstream of the German press is euro-friendly', he says.

Hughes Beaudouin of LC1/TF1 is with the mainstream in seeing the EU as a centre of power of which an account must be made. 'I've never been an enthusiast for the EU, but I'm not a sceptic; I think it's necessary, but it's an institution like others', he says. Brussels, from this point of view, is 'a centre of power, so we must pay attention to it'. It is still the place 'where one does Europe' but it is not the only one, as in Berlin and Paris decisions which were even more relevant have been taken. 'But here there's a concentration of power so it must be closely followed', he says.

Paradoxically, his cool approach towards the EU does not prevent him from being considered very pro-EU when in France. In public meetings, his fellow countrymen and countrywomen now regard even his neutrality and respect for the facts as suspiciously like propaganda – 'It's hard to explain why politics here is as it is – without appearing to be a spokesman for the EU', points out Beaudouin. This is particularly true in a moment where the public opinion is both more interested and more critical.

One of the reporters who appears to have thought most about the issue is Jean Quatremer of *Libération*, an exuberant, self-promoting, mercurial man. 'I myself am profoundly pro-European, I'm a federalist – but I'm a journalist first of all',[4] he says, recalling the numerous scandals he claims to have uncovered and the impact his work has had on the EU institutions. What makes the French journalist's work particularly unique in Brussels is that his reporting targets the EU elites more than his national politicians or his readership. Academic researchers have found it 'striking that journalists on the national and regional press attempt to influence EU institutions only "from time to time", to the same limited extent as regional and local interest groups, and even less than regional governments'.[5] Together with a few others, Quatremer does exactly the opposite: his relations with the EU institutions give prominence to his voice in the Brussels arena. Impartiality and objectivity, for those who share his approach, rely on the assumption that the EU is a good project in se. All the rest is there to be scrutinised.

But in France the country's role in the EU was not so controversial as it was, and still is, in the United Kingdom. EU reporting is not about taking sides, it is about 'bloody news' as Nick Robinson of the BBC told the King's College seminar – his employer being a news medium which is particularly concerned about objectivity. As we will see with the economic crisis in particular, the national narrative each country has on the EU has been flanked by a national agenda, which makes the judgement on what the 'bloody news' is and how it should be represented a matter of dispute. Robinson believes that in Brussels there is a permanent tension between two jobs: reporting institutions as they are and the permanent debate about legitimacy.

In the 2000s the BBC took a good deal of criticism for what was perceived as a sympathy for the EU; in 2005 an independent panel chaired by Lord Richard Wilson, the former head of the civil service, wrote in a mildly critical report that, notwithstanding its 'commitment to impartiality', the Corporation 'is not at present winning the battle for confidence in its coverage of EU news'.[6] In Wilson's words, there was 'no evidence of deliberate bias in BBC coverage of EU matters', but there is 'a widespread perception that it suffers from certain forms of cultural and unintentional bias'. This is a very problematic issue on which there is 'much agreement' even 'among groups who otherwise disagree passionately about almost everything else to do with Europe'. Wilson decided 'there is substance in their concern' and that there was something which felt 'like bias'. He concluded that there was a need to have 'better and more impartial coverage of the EU to explain major issues to a wider audience'.

According to the authors, the BBC needed to 'put in place effective arrangements for monitoring impartiality', namely the 'even-handed treatment of the broad spectrum of views held by the British electorate'.[7] Another criticism concerned the 'over simplified polarisation of issues and stereotyping', asking the broadcaster to 'be much more sophisticated in its presentation of different points of view on Europe'.[8]

Also, using 'Brussels' as a shortcut for the EU institutions 'contributes to a misleading impression' that the UK is not part of the decision-making process within EU institutions, according to the independent experts, who point out how the 'Westminster prism' through which the EU is reported can 'lead to the real story being neglected'. There are differences between the 'adversarial nature of British politics and the consensual nature of European politics'[9] which need to be further explained to the wider public. The BBC took the recommendations seriously and appointed a Europe Editor based in Brussels focusing on politics, policy, and economics of Europe and the European Union 'so as to give our audiences an authoritative overview of significant EU stories'.[10]

Wilson had discovered what the BBC itself later recognised: that its 'bias' towards the EU sprang from the largely unconscious attitudes of a journalistic staff broadly liberal or leftist in their views, reflecting the preference of that strand of opinion for greater EU integration to combat what is seen as narrow nationalism, or chauvinism. The report prompted the BBC to make changes in its EU coverage, putting some significant resources into it, though fewer than the German public networks ARD and ZDF, by some way the most serious broadcasters on the EU. At the King's College seminar, Nick Robinson said that the 2005 meeting of governors of the BBC had grasped both the need for more rigorous balance and objectivity, and for a much greater degree of regular coverage. But he also pointed out how the bias could be in both directions. In his view, there is a laziness in thinking that because the pro-EU people are wrong the Eurosceptics must be right, and vice versa. Robinson maintains that the crucial element in the 2005 meeting was exactly this: impartiality means neither to reflect the common wisdom, nor taking sides, and it is not up to the BBC to decide what acceptable views are.

In Eastern and Central European countries, the debate has not yet reached this stage, and Brussels still enjoys some prestige: though it varies widely from country to country. In the Czech Republic, a Eurobarometer survey in January 2014 showed only a little over a third holding favourable views of the Union, while only 19% thought Czech voices counted there: the turnout in the Europarliament elections in 2009, at 28%, was among the lowest. Jan Hornat, a researcher at the Forum 2000 organisation, writes that

> the Czech mainstream media often highlight and cling to the most 'foolish' and 'useless' EU directives and regulations (e.g. ban on classic light bulbs, parameters for chicken cages etc.) and fail to inform anyone about key EU legislation. This approach further strengthens the widespread impression that the European Parliament is a useless and costly institution [...] certain commentators and news outlets label the EU, 'the new Comecon' and claim that – through its directives and regulations – the EU aims to 'control every move' of European citizens.

Such allegations, implicitly comparing the EU to a communist organisation, feed Czech Eurosceptic moods.[11]

On the other hand, 'The EU is very popular [in Poland] not only as a eurozone, but because it gives Poland EU funds and a lot of money. It also gives us a kind of geo-political protection from Russia', says Tomasz Bielecki from Poland's *Gazeta Wyborcza*. However, its relative economic dynamism and insulation from the worst effects of the economic crisis have seen Poland take sides with Germany in the debate about austerity: 'We started to be the good people, with no recession and friends with Angela Merkel. So we feel as Northerners having trouble with the lazy Southerners.' According to the journalist, 'this is particularly remarkable if one thinks that Germans used to call *Polische Wirtschaft* [Polish business] all that was chaotic and messy'. But now the self-perception of the country has radically changed and the public opinion is less enthusiastic than before about the prospect of joining the euro. 'I think five years ago the majority was for joining the eurozone, and now it is only 30–40%.'

But being anti-EU for the Polish public does not mean 'that you want to leave the EU, but that you want to reform it'. The Polish are close to the British Tories, says Bielecki, when they say that they want to stay within the EU but they also want to 'reform it, or at least to stop more integration'. He cannot rule out, though, that in the future Polish Euroscepticism might grow.

Spain is notably one of the few countries untouched by Euroscepticism. The protests of the *indignados* movement which started in 2011 were one of the first vocal expressions of public discontent towards the EU policies, whose model has been followed by many throughout the EU, and their influence led to the unexpected success, at the EU elections, of the protest party 'Podemos', which is anti-austerity but not Eurosceptic. 'The instinct of most Spanish people is that EU problems have to be solved by the EU', says Bernardo de Miguel, Brussels correspondent for the Spanish business paper *Cinco Dias*. 'The owners of newspapers are pro-EU in general' and there are no 'Eurosceptics yet'. One of the reasons is that much of the blame public opinion put on the EU in other countries has been directed towards the austerity measures imposed in Spain. 'Now for the first time you can see journalists putting the blame on the EU or on Germany', says de Miguel.

Different shades of perplexity or scepticism existing in Continental Europe come across as an overall pro-EU approach (and thus 'automatically suspect') for the British reporter Chris Morris of the BBC. 'There is a good deal of cynicism and criticism about the way things are done – but it starts from the assumption that this is the way things are and should be. I don't think there's much thought about asking the big questions', he says. There are the institutional Europhiles, the opposition Europhiles, who both accept the terms of the dispute, and the radical anti-Europeans who, like extra-parliamentarian political organisations, project themselves as being outside of the existing debate and indicate a third way.

5

The Limits: The EU from 'Dull' to 'Crucial' in a Time of Crisis

> I felt a different responsibility, I was confronted [with] a
> different kind of expectation and fears.
>
> (Andrea Bonanni, *La Repubblica*)

Reporting the EU in the last five to six years has forced journalists to develop new skills and a wider understanding. As David Marsh puts it, during the EU crisis journalists, and not only European ones, found themselves in a situation where they 'only partly knew what they were looking at' and 'sometimes they barely knew at all'.[1] According to Marsh, 'conscientious' reporters made the effort to 'improve their expertise, to the length of taking courses, more frequently picking up, as journalists always do, from sources and more expert colleagues'. But was it really useful? As Marsh observes, 'deeper expertise is only a partial remedy' as 'it doesn't allow a depth of understanding, nor can it give long experience and knowledge of the likely actions and reactions of the major institutions and players'. In his view 'the trick is to become more widely expert – but to stop short of making a judgment'.[2]

Grasping the complexity of the EU story without getting lost in technicalities is challenging; all correspondents agree on that. This disorientation took two forms, both central to the acts of journalism which these correspondents were committing daily.

First, the place is wildly complex. It has 28 member states and three institutions: the EU Commission, with a commissioner from each of the 28 member states; the Parliament and its 751 elected members; and the Council of Ministers bringing together departmental ministers from all EU countries and the European Council, formed by the member states' presidents or prime ministers. Each commissioner has a directorate general behind him dealing with a range of highly technical and specialist areas, through macroeconomic indicators, finance, agriculture, regional, foreign and cultural policy. The Commission is based in Brussels and so is the Parliament, which also has another headquarters in Strasbourg where sessions are held every month, forcing MEPs and assistants to travel 430 km. The Council meets in Brussels, but every semester some of the meetings are held in the country which holds the rotating presidency, forcing journalists to travel there. Plus there are headquarters of some EU institutions in Luxembourg, about 200 km from Brussels, where meetings are held in April, June, and October. Luxembourg is home to the EU Court of Justice, while in Frankfurt, 430 km away from Brussels, is the European Central Bank. The latter sometimes has dedicated correspondents covering it, but in other cases they travel from elsewhere.

Brussels, Luxembourg, Strasbourg, Frankfurt: all house complex but crucial institutions which are part of what an EU correspondent has to learn and explain when s/he first arrives. Matthias Krupa of *Die Zeit*, who moved to Brussels in September 2011 after years as a political reporter in Germany, says that 'the first task here is to explain. The more I'm here the more I feel that.' Even when the readership is sophisticated, like that of *Die Zeit*, explaining the functioning of the European semester, namely a yearly cycle of economic and fiscal coordination among member states, can be very tricky. 'Yet you must explain it: it's where the money comes from,' says Krupa.

Topics like the European semester, crucial and highly technical, are easily upstaged by more inspiring yet less relevant stories. At the panel discussion on reporting the EU at King's College, *The Economist*'s John Peet pointed out that 'there is a problem about Brussels being boring'. The temptation for reporters and editors is to 'make up interesting stories', since 'it is much more fun to think the Commission is banning roast beef or olive oil on the table than following the progression of a directive'. In his view, 'the press could do more' to tackle an issue which has always existed but has become even more relevant: 'Europe is more complicated after the Lisbon Treaty.' That treaty became law at the end of 2009 and it revised the founding treaties by strengthening the role of the Parliament, creating the institutions of a President of the European Council and of a High Representative of the Union for Foreign Affairs. As a result, the central role once played by the Commission was diminished, while the Parliament and the Council gained more weight and influence.

This new scheme of power also altered one of the most common narrative devices of EU reporting: to identify the EU with the President of the Commission, widely seen as the most authoritative voice in Brussels. When Herman Van Rompuy was elected as President of the EU Council, it created a sort of diarchy which was complicated to explain to the wider public. One of the most basic exercises of EU journalists, looking for comments from the EU institutions on all sorts of national or international news, became confusing. A comment by President Barroso would be followed by one by Van Rompuy, sometimes showing little unity, sometimes repeating the same words.

'It is a very difficult story to cover', says George Parker, the *FT*'s Political Editor and formerly its Bureau Chief in Brussels. 'Brussels is a city with faceless buildings, faceless people with foreign unpronounceable names, and they make decisions at a snail's pace. This is not appealing for editors at a time when newspaper sales have been collapsing.' Luigi Ippolito, the foreign editor at *Corriere della Sera*, is similarly sharp: 'The main issue with Brussels is that it is a boring story. How can you get excited about the economy, that sad science? Because they are boring, institutions are not much covered.' At the same time, their interference in the national life of the 28 member states cannot be ignored and has to be explained properly. The space it gets in the printed press is limited: the most successful correspondents are those who are able to give a lively account of what goes on. This does not solve the problem entirely. Griselda Pastor, the correspondent for Cadena Ser Radio of Spain, put it succinctly – 'concerning Europe, the more you explain, the less you inspire love'.

'Boring' can be the way in which journalists describe 'complicated': but the first adjective is accurate insofar as journalists know that their readers – much more so today, with a hundred different media choices every minute – would have in the main a very limited patience with articles describing in detail the policies, legislative projects, and debates over technical issues. Still, they would complain about the lack of information about Brussels and vote accordingly: the lack of transparency from EU institutions is often mentioned as one of the main reasons of distrust.

Journalism shaped for wide sections of the general public must use personality, polemic, and a strong narrative drive to engage audiences: the use of these tools in reporting on the workings of the EU is severely limited. The largest obstacle to understanding what is happening in the institutions of the Union which play a very large role in determining the public framework to our lives is the general lack of interest in them.

The second and more contemporary factor is the need, on the part of the reporters in Brussels, to understand what was happening when the various waves of crisis rolled over them from the late 2000s on, coming on top of a beat which many confess they can at best pick at – often gathering, of necessity, the lower hanging fruit. Many did, as David Marsh writes in *Europe's Deadlock*, go to the lengths of taking courses in finance; more often they picked it up from the more informed. But, as Marsh also says, they did not then become all-knowing: the layers of complexity and of political calculation are so many and so deep that to make a prediction is more foolhardy for a journalist in this context than it is in other, relatively more comprehensible areas.

For most of the reporters, the debt crisis started at the end of 2009 when the newly elected government in Greece revealed the real state of the country's finances. The news media, in the main, stopped wondering whether the eurozone was on the brink of collapse in the summer of 2012, when the ECB intervened with the statement from its president, Mario Draghi, that he would defend the currency with 'whatever it takes'. Between these two events, all the usual issues faced by Brussels correspondents met with a sudden, often uncontrollable acceleration: what was then perceived as boring became necessary, and the old technicalities not only became all the more technical, but turned into something of vital importance for every EU citizen. Each journalist had to find his way in order to convey a difficult, crucial piece of information. 'I felt a different responsibility, I was confronted with a different kind of expectation and fears,' says Andrea Bonanni.

The crisis was not totally unexpected: or at least, there were straws in the wind, though none strong enough to justify reporting going from normal record-keeping to crisis. Bernardo de Miguel says:

> In 2004 Pedro Solbes [a former European Commissioner and finance and economy minister, 2004–9 in the socialist government of Jose Zapatero] said that the housing sector was not stable and he tried to pinch the bubble; in 2003 someone like [Miguel] Ordonez [a former Spanish official and governor of the Bank of Spain, 2006–12], was already aware of the issues and wrote them in an article, but then there were the elections and everything was silenced.

He adds that 'we already knew at the time that the figures coming from Greece were faulty' and at the very beginning it was 'hard to grasp the consequences of the deficit in Greece, because when something happens for a second time you think you have a precedent'.

Why did the press not raise an alarm over what was going on? Why didn't they keep their eyes open? Brussels, sometimes, 'is like a bubble', says de Miguel, where you don't always have the exact measure of what is going on in the outside world. When in 2009 the Dubai property market crashed, wiping 50% off the value of properties and revealing large financial weaknesses in a range of state-owned companies, 'it was difficult to make the link' with Greece and understand it would be a powerful trigger for the instability on the markets.

Between 2009 and 2012 a huge number of emergency EU summits took place, representing a physical challenge as well as an intellectual one for journalists. There was an increasing demand for reporting and for analysis, but the work became increasingly arduous. Scenarios which were barely imaginable just one year before had to be seriously taken into consideration. 'It was very important to have your own information and your own string to follow', says Philippe Ricard, who thinks that the story was so complicated that it needed teams of reporters working on it – yet at the same time, the story could be broken into too many pieces, and run the risk of becoming incoherent. Simultaneously, the material handled by journalists was often explosive, capable of causing large disturbances in national policies and in markets. 'One needed to work on every single option and that meant that you could not rule out things that could be damaging for the markets. Responsibility does not mean to hide things; one had to avoid self-censorship', says Ricard.

Contemplating options which were unimaginable before was one of the most challenging aspects of reporting about the crisis. Decades of customary practices and beliefs were swept away by the events. 'Some very good sources let me know that a partial restructuring of the Greek debt was about to happen', recalls Federico Fubini, while admitting the 'psychological resistance' which prevented him from breaking the news. Andrea Bonanni, who had covered the collapse of the Soviet Union and says that, even now, it remains by far the biggest story he has ever covered, says that in that case you knew 'what was happening', whereas with the debt crisis 'you had to guess all the time' and answer large questions like: 'Will the euro survive?' He adds, 'I was absolutely sure it would have survived', because 'all the alternatives were just worse.'

According to Bernardo de Miguel, 'the message we received is that never ever would the IMF come to the eurozone, we were the wealthiest continent in the world, but then in February 2010 everything changed and we understood that this time it would be different'. Received wisdom, instead of being the usual reassuring guidance, became an obstacle to understanding.

Each journalist had to set his own target in reporting. 'My first two objectives are that the reader has to understand and that he has to make a step forward compared to what he reads usually', says Federico Fubini, who wrote for *Il Corriere della Sera* and now is at *La Repubblica*. 'Those are new, unfamiliar arguments, quite hard to understand, so I think it is important not to tell more than two important ideas at a time', he says.

In his view it is also important to remain cautious and to be 'very well briefed' in order to make one's reporting bulletproof from polemic and criticisms. What is particularly tricky about the EU, he says, is the lack of a 'direct interlocutor', namely the fact that it is always a very composite story. For Matina Stevis, from *Dow Jones-Wall Street Journal*, 'the main problem is the fragmented nature of the stories' and the complacent tendency to listen to only one version. 'You cannot run a story that comes from the Commission, you have to understand the nature of the beast', she says, 'because all the institutions involved will try to feed you with stories most of the time.'

The crisis proved to be a good opportunity to improve the coverage of the EU, or at least to increase it. 'It was impossible not to open the news with an EU story at least three times a week and this has given us the advantage of greater continuity', says SkyTG24's Giovanna Pancheri. Says the BBC's Chris Morris: 'It was exhausting. The *Today* programme would do a two-way at 6.30 [a.m.] with correspondents and I was there almost every day for months', he says, thinking in particular about the 'white heat of the summer of 2012'.

'Journalism is a first draft of history, but the story was far bigger than expected and many of the drafts were pretty flawed', says Toby Vogel from *European Voice*. 'The main challenge was to understand the detail but without being lost in technicalities, and without losing sight of the political consequences', says Bernardo de Miguel. In his view 'it has been easier than ever to write about the crisis' because for once the story was there and you did not have to beg for attention from the editors and the readers. 'Most of the media understood the issue at stake was not Greece or Portugal, but the eurozone', he says, recalling a time of unprecedented attention to an EU story.

6

Living in Financial Times: Getting to Grips with Financial Complexity

> All the means we had before have disappeared. We do not travel any more, we cannot go anywhere. You cannot be where things take place.
>
> (Griselda Pastor Llopart, Cadena Ser)

The euro crisis meant that the economic and financial content of Brussels correspondents' reporting not only increased, but it became at times fearsomely technical and came with the urgency that would become the trademark of their work in the succeeding years. The credit crisis of Northern Rock – a British bank, based in Newcastle, which suffered a bank run in 2007 – was the first event of the sort to be covered, but it concerned only a limited number of journalists. In September 2008 the collapse of Lehman Brothers happened during the French rotating presidency of the EU. Nicolas Sarkozy, president at the time, called several emergency meetings among EU leaders in order to decide how to rescue the severely impaired European banking system. This was not limited to the eurozone and, with hindsight, looked like a rehearsal for what was about to happen.

'In February 2010, I became an economic correspondent,' says Tomasz Bielecki of *Gazeta Wyborcza*. This sudden career change happened to almost every single correspondent in Brussels when the newly elected Greek government between 2009 and 2010 revealed the true state of the country's public deficit and the eurozone started shaking violently. The press used the same tools it had used before: it covered the overnight emergency meetings, listened to the crescendo of measures which were being adopted to contain the crisis, and very soon realised this was unlike any other thing they had reported about before.

'At the beginning you do not understand much from a technical point of view' and this, says Griselda Pastor Llopart, can have serious consequences in terms of being able to question power: 'For instance, at the end of a council late at night authorities said they were about to take money from the bank accounts of Cyprus. This was so unbelievable that it took me some time to realise what they were doing and I thought "but they must know what they are doing". Then I realised how serious and unprecedented it was,' she recalls, regretting she was not ready to ask the right question, at the right moment.

'Some extraordinarily important decisions were being made at 3 a.m., when everyone was knackered', says the BBC's Chris Morris – and he extends the description to the politicians who had to make decisions, as well as to the journalists who reported them. 'This is the way that the EU works – but I think it's true, as a senior official once told me, that you could go round the table of the European Council of Ministers and half of them wouldn't know what they were talking about.' During the euro crisis, some extremely technical and very expensive decisions were being taken.

On the night between 9 and 10 May 2010, a €750bn fund was created to prevent the eurozone from breaking up. Reporting about the decision required not only a daring imagination, as in a single night more taboos about the EU were broken than in ten years of history, but also a remarkable familiarity with financial vehicles, stability mechanisms, and government-backed guarantees.

Most journalists interviewed were not trained as economists or financial specialists: they speak of a 'steep learning curve' which they had to undergo, usually by picking up information from specialist colleagues or contacts, in some cases through taking courses in economics and finance. 'I took a course on financial regulation and other issues – I had no economic background: I am a generalist,' says Hughes Beaudouin of LCI/TF1, pointing out how the final outcome – clarity and precision – is always difficult to achieve. 'The hardest thing here is to find experts who can explain clearly – and when you aren't an expert yourself, it's difficult to judge who is good, who not. And as well, you must also find someone who's good on TV.'

For Alain Franco, a French freelance journalist who has reported for many media outlets, the task is to be 'simple but not simplistic' even when you are 'submerged by ultra-technical issues'. Franco works for Swiss Radio, 'which is like the *FT* of radios, as we mainly speak to bankers', and he reckons that his media allowed him a lot of space, particularly at night, when there was no competition from other news, the meetings were still going on, and he had the time to explain decisions. The learning curve is not over, of course. 'I have grasped it is complex and I grasp more of its complexity every day, but there is more to learn every day', says Anton La Guardia, who wrote the weekly Charlemagne column for *The Economist*.

'The tempo of the story has been given by the markets', sighs Philippe Ricard while recollecting the years he spent covering the crisis. The sense of emergency, the countless meetings which were dubbed 'the last resort summit', the obsessive control of communications were due first and foremost to the high reactivity of the markets, which were imposing their hectic rhythm. 'If we had followed only the markets, the eurozone would have disappeared', according to the *Le Monde* correspondent, who points out how 'for three years we had a very intense, a very captivating job'. Which had, in his view, a historical importance: 'I think that for many journalists of my generation it has been the biggest story they ever covered.'

Like any other EU economic sector, the media had to undergo austerity cuts too. Brussels, once home to the biggest press room in the world in terms of accredited journalists, saw the number of full-time correspondents shrink because of the economic crisis and, first and foremost, because of the crisis of the sector. Many journalists turned into freelancers. 'The press representation in Brussels grew strongly for some years – then began to cut back in the past decade. And so there was a paradox – as the financial crisis grew, the news media bureaux shrank, because of the media crisis', says Paul Taylor of Reuters. Not only was the topic more demanding to follow, but in order to appease the markets, many of the meetings took place during the weekends or at night, making life quite hard for the media. Nearly all say that they are much more stretched, and at times work round the clock.

Freelancers and stringers, they say, very often do not have the time to analyse things, nor the weight to have their byline on a story published. When they are based in capitals like Berlin their work is not considered useful for EU reporting as they 'don't usually write about EU affairs', according to Bernardo de Miguel. 'Of course they can learn, but it still takes time', he says. Griselda Pastor says that 'the young contributors write on demand from the central offices and, for what they are being paid, they copy newswires'. In order to have an edge on the others in covering the crisis, it is necessary to have someone who has the time to find sources and to cultivate them, according to correspondents. 'The tricky part is that before in Brussels you had first-hand news. Now the focus of the news is coming from Berlin and Frankfurt', says de Miguel, explaining that only one Spanish newspaper, *La Vanguardia*, has a real correspondent in Berlin.

Choosing good freelancers, paying them well, and giving them the confidence to make suggestions and create relationships is a mandatory step for the survival of quality journalism even in hard times. But as things are now, what de Miguel and Pastor lament is the lack of teamwork.

Chris Morris, with one of the world's largest broadcaster's resources behind him, reckons that 'I would still struggle with the really complex matters of the banking unions, but then we have specialists in London who can do it from there – we're atypical and lucky in that.' He mentions the case of Arthur Beesley, the former Brussels correspondent for the *Irish Times*, 'who was alone – it was a huge story for Ireland – and he was exhausted'. But Beesley, like many others whose country was in the eye of the storm, had no choice but to learn as quickly as possible and keep up with the hectic pace of the news.

The issue was also very acute for those reporters who had been sent by their news organisation with little experience, little specialised knowledge, and little backup from their base. Tomasz Bielecki of *Gazeta Wyborcza* – the daily edited since its foundation in 1989, as communism was breaking down, by the former dissident and Solidarity militant Adam Michnik – came to Brussels in autumn 2009. Revealing the slenderness of resources in the most important newspaper in a state of nearly 40 million people, Bielecki noted:

> I started writing editorials in 2011. Two reasons – first, I learned much more about Europe; second, one of my predecessors [in Brussels] left the paper, and there are few specialists on the EU left – so they had to ask me. Five or six years ago the situation was better – but some left, and some were fired. Gazeta [its circulation, over 600,000 at its peak ten years ago, is now under 200,000] has no money to hire new specialists.

At the height of the crisis reporters had to do more than one job, considering both the big picture and the details. At least access to information was not hard for Bielecki, unlike in Moscow. 'There is no access to the Kremlin, not even for the *New York Times*', he says, adding that 'the Russian press don't have briefings and their reporting is based on speculation. I needed a week to arrange a phone conversation with the spokesperson of a minister.' In Brussels it is quite the opposite: 'You have to defend yourself from spokespeople.'

While Poland's interest in the crisis was limited – for the Poles, the Eastern partnership was much more important, for instance – for Spain and Greece the issue was very different. Journalists had to cover a story which affected their countries greatly with fewer resources than most, a disturbing fact.

The most dramatic case is that of Greece, where austerity measures imposed in exchange for the bailouts had an inevitable impact on an already fragile media sector. Talk of Greece leaving the eurozone has been a recurrent feature of the last four years and the Greeks have been targeted by campaigns by some German media, *Bild* in particular. Arguably Greece should have the most informed and active news media in order to assist its 11.3 million people to understand something of what is happening to them, and thus make more informed choices on what brand of politics to support and what measures they themselves might be able take to avoid the worst effects of the crisis. It doesn't.

'There were fifteen Greek correspondents at the Commission, but now there are only three or four who can make a living from journalism,' says Vangelis Demeris, an experienced freelance for Greek and Cypriot media who recently wrote *La face cachée de la crise grecque* (The Hidden Face of the Greek Crisis) to explain to an international audience what were the issues at stake.[1] 'We have many jobs, but none pays more than €1,000 a month and we never know what the next month will look like,' he says.

The Greek case is quite singular, but worth understanding in a little more depth because it illuminates something of the same problems faced by other small or smaller countries whose journalists are inexperienced and whose news media are run much more for profit, or for status, or for the influence they can have on the government than for any public service ideals. The Greek news media were not well developed before the crisis burst, and have proven at best weak in providing a good service of news and analysis during it. In 1989, later than in other European countries, the state-owned broadcasting channels which had held a monopoly of TV and radio broadcasting (three channels in each) were forced by the government to cede ground to independent broadcasters.

Despina Trivolis, former editor of the *BH Magazine* published by the daily *To Vima* (on whose work for the Reuters Institute for the Study of Journalism much of this description is based), characterises the period from 1989 to 2005 as 'the era of the bubble', in which the media underwent huge growth. At its height, no fewer than 39 national daily newspapers and dozens of TV and radio stations were founded – most of which were the property of business people who wished to use them to either put pressure on, or to support, the state.

A Reuters investigation in December 2012 claimed that 'per capita, Greece has far more national newspaper titles than, say, Germany or the UK. The country also has nine national TV stations, six of them privately owned, and numerous private radio stations.'[2] These figures might argue for a diverse and lively, democratic *agora* of news and opinion: but they don't. Freedom House, in its annual index on press freedom, accords the Greek news media the status of only 'partly free'. 'How can all these media outlets operate profitably? They don't. They are subsidized by their owners who, while they would welcome any income from media sales, use the media primarily to exercise political and economic influence,' says a 2006 cable from the US Embassy in Athens obtained by Wikileaks and quoted by Reuters.

Trivolis says that 30% of the advertisements come from the state – and that these advertisements were placed on political grounds, not on criteria derived from circulation figures. *Chora*, a daily paper with a circulation of some 800 a day and 2,000 on Sunday, received in most years more than €3 million from state advertising notwithstanding its poor readership. The 'networks of corruption' – as the Reuters 2012 investigation characterised much of the Greek media's relationships with government and corporations – meant that most of the media houses were highly indebted. However, the banks would not demand payment or foreclose, afraid of revelations about their own business.

Most journalists, says Trivolis, receive skeleton or no wages. In addition to this, there is 'little real reporting but lots of conspiracy theories', which does not help in building credibility for them or a solid basis for citizens to analyse their situation. Journalists are seen as compromised by their connections to the state and to wealthy corporations – and are at times attacked in the street, or are the object of demonstrations. The most prominent case is the one of Costas Vaxevanis, an investigative journalist who published a list, provided by the then French Finance Minister Christine Lagarde to the Greek authorities, containing the names of Greek citizens who had moved their wealth to Switzerland in order to dodge taxes. The authorities made no use of it and Vaxevanis went on trial, was acquitted, but then faced trial again.[3] Tax dodging in Greece is endemic: according to the Greek Treasury, at the end of November 2013 the state was owed €63bn in unpaid taxes. According to 2009 figures from Helvea SA, there were about €35bn of Greek money in Swiss banks.[4]

This is the home context in Athens for Greece's few and overstretched Brussels correspondents. They must attempt to explain the actions – or inaction – of the institutions of the EU, institutions which many of their fellow citizens believe are depriving them of the necessary resources to recover from the crisis. 'The media can be either pro or against euro: it's a very Manichaean, black-or-white situation,' Demeris says.

The EU authorities, anxious about the fate of the many billions they have advanced to Greece, intrude deeply into public life. 'The role of the press is to try to explain why the austerity measures are inevitable,' says Demeris, who thinks that 'a critical eye' as well as 'transparency' are of the utmost importance. 'Among the journalists, I have been very pro-European: we cannot change the rules afterwards.' Being European means that 'there is a need for more solidarity and there is a need for growth,' he says. But apart from any ideological point of view, he believes that the responsibility of the Brussels correspondent of a Greek news medium is to set out the facts first and foremost. 'Every correspondent is a vehicle of truth,' he says. 'Those who have tried to cover Europe from Athens have made many mistakes; the work of a correspondent here is partly about having to fight with your editor in chief to impose a version of events that is not the one conveyed by national newswires.' This can be delusional and create further confusion in a country that needs none. 'Europe is very negative in the Greek press, there is always a new hysteria,' he says.

Since 2010 Greece – the cradle of Western theatre as well as of philosophy and democracy – has been represented in the news media irresistibly as a theatre where the end of the democracy has been staged – the human and painfully emotional counterpart to cold, technocratic Brussels. In no other country has the public display of anger and despair been as vivid as Greece: the constant demonstrations, the extreme behaviour of the fascist Golden Dawn party, the cliff-edge votes to sustain the centrist government, all lend themselves to a more immediate and exciting coverage than the technicalities of bailouts or discussions on financial integration. Television channels round the world loved Athens in turmoil, and gave the story much more attention than the less televisual situations in Portugal and Ireland.

Some media, like *Dow Jones-Wall Street Journal*, increased their coverage of Athens by hiring people like Matina Stevis, a young Greek with degrees from Oxford and the London School of Economics who used to write for *Eleftherotypia* from London. She covers the EU and Greece while being Brussels-based. 'When I go to Athens for work, I tend to stay in a hotel not to be too influenced by my family point of view and to try to keep a distance,' she says. Everyone in Greece is 'touched by the crisis' and it is easy to become very emotional and angry about the situation. That's why it is even more important to have a 'system that balances your biases', a newspaper where there is 'a clear separation between facts and opinions'. At the same time, Stevis maintains, 'it is good to bring the expertise that comes from your knowledge of a situation. In this sense I feel that I am doing something useful for my country.'

Since the beginning of the crisis, the most positive development for journalism was the need, which the crisis forced upon correspondents, to connect what happened (or did not happen) at the core of the union with what was happening in the periphery. Enriching EU reporting with an understanding of what was going on in at least some of the member states and cities allowed the journalists, and their audiences, to start grasping Europe as a whole. The previous EU 'meetings tourism' – flying to a city with other journalists, going from the hotel to a remote conference centre without talking to people – was replaced by an attempt to understand how other member states worked.

Even so, many EU correspondents believe that the social aspects of the crisis were not covered promptly enough. It took some time before people understood that it was not 'just a financial crisis – it's a human, political, social crisis too – and a newspaper like mine treats it as such', says Quatremer of *Libération*. 'We have correspondents in other capitals – but the problem is that I have the technical knowledge.' As a step towards a better understanding and reporting of the issues at stake with the EU project, it would be desirable for journalists to travel more and not just to their country. 'To cover this properly you must have an open mind and ask the big questions – such as, what are you doing, cutting the wages of the officials? Have you, Mr Rehn [Olli Rehn, the Economics Commissioner], been in Greece where an official gets €2,000 euros a month – and it's cut to €1,400 a month – and he has a mortgage of €1,000 a month – how is he to live – how do you, sir, explain that?' asks Quatremer.

Spain, with media far less compromised and with more resources than those of Greece, had nevertheless seen a huge slump in the property market and a rise in unemployment to an estimated one in four out of work, nearly one in two among the youth. Most media have had to bear large cuts in staff and journalists' expenses: Griselda Pastor of Cadena Ser Radio says that 'all the means we had before have disappeared. We do not travel any more, we cannot go anywhere. The majority of people cannot even go to Ecofin [the Finance ministers' gathering] meetings that are held abroad. You cannot be where things take place.' The pressure of events and the limited time and even more limited resources mean, she says, that 'by Cadena Ser the social side has not been covered', even though the social issues have been considerable: 'This is not a normal society we are talking about, but a society on the way to destruction. We have a new class which is "lumpen-social", but it is not something we can talk about.'

7

Video Games: The Challenges for TV Journalists and the Role of 'Mass' Media

> Man getting out of car walking into building, man walking out of building getting into car.
>
> (Chris Morris, BBC)

The European Union manages to be even less eloquent with images than with words. Covering the Brussels institutions is a particular challenge for TV journalists, who have to summarise a complex message and have only dull, grey buildings to help them illustrate the story. But TV is the main source of news in nearly all countries, of whatever form of government, and their mass audience is often less knowledgeable than that of print media. This means that fewer things can be taken for granted and there is a need for simpler concepts, clear and short explanations, which leads some to believe that TV is not the appropriate medium to deal with EU affairs.[1]

The need for pictures and at least some drama finds in EU coverage one of its largest challenges: everything is complex, most of what is important happens in private and the pictures presented are, as Chris Morris of the BBC puts it, 'man getting out of car walking into building, man walking out of building getting into car'. No wonder that the EU institutions were upstaged by the protests in the squares of the EU member states and that the liveliness of the latter had a more striking impact on the viewer's imagination. In order to preserve the attractiveness of the television news, everyone seems to agree that some rules have to be followed. To avoid using too many images coming from the institutions seems to be the first and most important.

TV, still the mass media *par excellence*, very often has to fight against tabloid newspapers as its main competitors in those countries where tabloids exist. This is less the case in France, Spain, and Italy (though it is changing there, as the political forces try on the Eurosceptic clothes), more in Germany and especially in the UK, where some sections of the print press are particularly opinionated when it comes to the EU. The pre-eminence of public service broadcasters has been increasingly challenged by commercial news in recent decades and as Paschal Preston points out, 'the relative roles of PSB services have declined significantly in most EU countries compared to the situation some 10 or 20 years ago'.[2]

This adds a degree of difficulty to the work of TV journalists, since the often highly polemical opinions expressed by tabloids may be trusted by the public, who expect to see them reflected in the TV coverage. Those who dislike and distrust the EU most can mistake an objective description of its actions for pro-EU bias. This does not make the EU easier to report. The BBC European correspondent, Chris Morris, points out how unpalatable the institutions are from a TV point of view. Some of them, like the Parliament, are so for structural reasons like the need for translations – 'It is terrible to picture. When someone tells a joke you can hear the laughter ripple round the room in stages till at last the Latvians in a corner get it.'

TV reporters also find the approach to TV disappointingly ham-fisted. On the day in September 2013 on which we attended the press briefing, the former Dutch Cabinet Minister Neelie Kroes, the Commissioner for the Digital Agenda, had illuminated a point she wished to make about the use of digital technology in schools by producing a schoolgirl at the regular noon press briefing, to speak on the advantages of the digital blackboard. Morris was indignant: 'Did they really put that on for TV? Don't they realise that if they wanted it on TV they should arrange to go back to her school and film it there where you could see what she was talking about?'

His verdict as a TV journalist on the midday briefing is quite blunt: 'There's nothing they can really do to get us interested in the press conference', which is a 'complete waste of time'. This is mainly due to the fact that spokespersons cannot focus when they have so many requests at a time. 'Say there's a story about agriculture. There would be someone from the BBC who would want a simple explanation of the issue to put into a TV or radio package,' says Morris. 'Then there would be someone from *South West Farming Monthly* who needs an answer to a very specific question about which cows are going to be moved from one field to another. And so the PRs have so much to cover that they often end up saying nothing.'

Even before the beginning of the debt crisis, TV journalists tried to get out of Brussels as much as possible and to focus on people-centred stories and a more human approach. 'TV is about pictures, you can't tell a story without getting pictures other than the Berlaymont,' says Morris, who points out that 'there is an inbuilt assumption that stories about the EU are boring' and that in order 'to persuade the news desks that it is not so' journalists have to make 'a fairly insistent point about getting out of Brussels'. Every news story coming from the EU needs to be illustrated by a concrete example, or by a tailor-made explanation. 'If for example I'm working on data protection, I'll ask for a briefing with the data protection spokesman rather than sitting at a briefing hearing two minutes on this and two on that', he points out. 'A lot of it is verbal diarrhoea.'

The issues faced by Morris are very common among Brussels TV correspondents. Giovanna Pancheri accepts the old journalistic cliché that 'if it bleeds, it leads'. The EU usually 'bleeds' only when there is a crisis or when it is perceived as being on the brink of collapse. 'Europe has never been an interesting story, a homicide is much better,' she says, mentioning two weaknesses of the EU: 'the issues are very complex' so that 'you always have to keep it very simple', and 'the EU is non-existent from a visual point of view'. The positive side of the debt crisis is that 'the public opinion has understood that simple decisions have real repercussions' and that the viewers finally got acquainted with some technical terms which do not need lengthy explanations any more.

Hughes Beaudouin, who broadcasts continually for LC1/TF1 because of the interest French viewers have in some EU topics like agriculture, finds that the internal workings of the EU are hard to get across on TV. 'There are visible powers and invisible powers', he says, pointing out how far the European decision-making is from the French one. 'To explain the lobbies in France is complicated, and the lobbies have a lot of influence on decisions, they are integral to the system', he says, adding: 'we have a system where the President decides and the Parliament validates – here there are many powers which balance each other and must negotiate all the time'. Plus, there is a lack of TV characters. Chris Morris made a similar point: 'It is hard to cover Parliament because TV needs personalities – and unlike in the UK but like other national parliaments in Europe there are not the gladiatorial battles, Prime Minister's Questions.'

The debate over what TV can and cannot do has continued for the six decades in which it has become an increasingly powerful force. For the French sociologist, the late Pierre Bourdieu,

access to television exerts in return a massive censorship, a loss of
autonomy stemming from, among other things, the fact that the subject
under discussion is imposed, the way in which the communication is
conducted is imposed and above all, that the lack of time imposes on the
discussion such constraints that it's very unlikely that anything can be
said.[3]

For the Political Editor of Sky UK, Adam Boulton, however, the brevity
which TV imposes in the form of politicians' or TV pundits' sound bites
are the necessary outcome of a marketplace of huge media choice and 'if
your message is good enough to be heard over all of that, it's probably
good enough – full stop'. Besides, he writes, 'there is more in-depth
political discussion readily available than ever before' – discussion which
sound bites prompt, and to which they lead an audience.[4]

The coverage of the EU is one of the many subsets of that debate: and
that coverage demonstrates that *both* of the core contentions of Bourdieu
and Boulton are true. The form of TV journalism – and often of discussion
programmes – does impose tight constraints on what can be said: yet at the
same time the telegraphic style of TV pieces with their sound bites can
signal to those interested the need to learn more, hear more argument –
which is more available now through the internet than ever before. There is
no debate, however, that TV news is a series of brief items: that the
constraint, of on average two-minute pieces (except in rare cases of very
large events which demand longer treatment), is brutal on detail, nuance
and alternative explanations; and that the normal coverage, with explanation
necessarily kept to a minimum, is likely to mean little to those who don't
care to be informed about the nature, main actors, and issues of the EU.

The temptation would be to blame the public, but that would also be
a way to admit a failure. Broadcasters, especially public broadcasters, are
under an obligation to produce information which is at once informative,
accurate, and vivid: new graphic techniques can aid this. Brussels is just
like any other political and economic capital, but TV correspondents
cannot rely on the feeling of familiar and recognisable power that Downing
Street in London or the Elysée in Paris will prompt in viewers. The
structure of what needs to be told might be similar, but everything needs
to be explained: nothing can be taken for granted. The nature of the
institutions, with their deliberate lack of drama, their substitution of
expertise and regulations agreed in closed-door meetings of the European
Council of heads of state for open and often exciting debate, imposes a

complexity on the project which only those professionally engaged in its activities will make the effort to understand.

Yet, as the past few years have shown, the EU is central to the European economies, to their social provisions, and the very way of life of the European citizens. There is a limit to how attractive broadcasters can make the issues which are the stuff of the European Union's institutions: a working knowledge of their activities and importance requires – as do national political systems – a willingness to make the intellectual effort to understand and, only after that, make a judgement.

A partial antidote to the paucity of TV coverage of the EU has been Euronews, created in 1993 with headquarters in Lyon. 'It started after the first Gulf war, with the arrival of all news channels and the overwhelming presence of CNN in the media sector,' recalls Annalisa Piras, who used to edit the *Europe* programme for Euronews at its beginning. 'The project had been in the drawers for years, but it came to life with Delors and with the impulse given by Maastricht', she says, pointing out that difficulties quickly emerged because the different national broadcasters did not agree on the basics. 'The Brits immediately withdrew their support, and the biggest impulse came from RAI and France Television. The CNN perspective was unashamedly American, while for Euronews the main difficulty was to figure out how to cover EU news knowing that in each country the items would have a very different degree of relevance.'

Its mission is to cover world news from a pan-European perspective: it broadcasts in the main languages of the European Union, as well as Russian, Ukrainian, Turkish, Arabic, and Persian. Its main shareholders are France Televisions (24%), Radiotelevisione Italiana (21.5%), All Russian State TV and Radio (17%), and the Turkish TV and Radio Corporation (15.7%). 'It is the largest and most widespread transnational media in the world', which presents some obvious challenges. 'We needed to reflect thoroughly on what was news', recalls Piras, who was responsible for the first daily bulletins entirely dedicated to the EU. 'We would cover stories from the EU institutions only if they were relevant for European citizens' in a very objective way, explaining the consequences on people's lives of a decision taken in Brussels.

The European Commission tripled its contribution to the €60m running costs in 2011 to €15m, allowing the channel to open 11 new offices: the remainder of the income is from advertising and licence fees. It claims a reach of 170 million households in Europe and 35 million in 155 countries worldwide: and it also claims an audience of some 2.6 million for a service which is mainly rolling news in half-hour segments. Its style is restrained, with voice-overs in different languages to filmed reports: it has been frequently accused of broadcasting 'propaganda' for the EU – most trenchantly by the Swedish-based Timbro think tank, whose *The European Union Burden*[5] sees the channel as part of a much larger publicity machine bent on persuading Europeans of the need for ever closer union.

'We never had any editorial control from the EU', Piras maintains, pointing out that the 'editorial line was clear from the beginning, and those who work for Euronews of course believe in the historical importance of the EU project'. But it does not mean becoming the house organ of the Commission, an accusation she dismisses, saying that it is 'just like accusing a political reporter of being in favour of Westminster'. Overcoming the debate 'between Europe or non Europe' does not mean being partisan.

8

Absent Enemies: Reporting on Brussels out of Brussels

> Many media are absolutely superficial in the way they report about EU news, without understanding how much they end up influencing the political class in their decision-making.
>
> (David Carretta, *Il Foglio*)

Reporters in Brussels influence both politicians and the public in a very pronounced way: and they do so, as everywhere, within an assumed framework – in the case of the EU, a framework of approval or disapproval, support or opposition, for or against. The institutions of the EU are, for nearly all the reporters' audiences, so mysterious and complex that a strongly presented simplification – for or against – can carry considerable weight, and strongly influence both the general public and the political and other elites.

One of the largest claims of influencing the political class through public perception which we know of is that of Boris Johnson, now Mayor of London (see Appendix 1). In the early 1990s he was the *Telegraph*'s correspondent in Brussels. In his biography of Delors,[1] Charles Grant, a fellow correspondent of Johnson's in Brussels, writes that an article by Johnson which became the front-page splash in the *Sunday Telegraph* – 'Delors Plan to Rule Europe', widely reprinted in Denmark's newspapers – helped tip a vote on the Maastricht Treaty towards the rejectionist camp in July 1992, with a 50.7 majority. The next year Denmark was granted various opt-outs, including to keep the krone, its currency, and eventually ratified the Treaty. Johnson boasted later: 'I probably did contribute to the Danish rejection of Maastricht.'[2]

To be dramatic, funny, flimsy, and therefore effective, it is better not to take the topic too seriously. 'Some papers have a deliberate policy of not having someone in Brussels', says George Parker. 'If you have a reporter based in Brussels you can see the two sides of the story' and 'the day you try to explain to your editor that things are more complicated than they seem is the day you are brought back to England ... the *Mail* and *Sun* tried to have a correspondent there but they only lasted a few months.' Parker says he is trapped in the paradox of being regarded as tough on the EU authorities and thus 'Eurosceptic' in Brussels, and as a strong pro-European in London. Even though he is not a 'starry-eyed' Europhile, he points out that 'Brussels is not running Britain on a day by day basis' and it is a 'wilful damage perpetrated on the readers not getting the other side of the story'. But who wants a sophisticated and well-argued form of Euroscepticism when there is a far more entertaining version readily available?

Paul Taylor of Reuters says that 'Many news media and many countries don't cover the EU at all with their own correspondents. Almost all the UK media withdrew, for example: mainly on cost grounds, I believe, but also because they thought their audiences had little interest.' Taylor says that the aim of the Eurosceptic press is not to present reasoned arguments against a project, but rather to demolish it through funny, unlikely stories. 'For some, those who were strongly opposed to what the EU did, they didn't want the facts to get in the way of a good story,' he says, adding: 'They use stringers or send someone when they want to do a piece. Even the BBC cut back: part of that was cost cutting, but I also think it was because some of their stars, like Steven Sackur (who now chairs the *Hard Talk* programme) or Mark Mardell (presently the BBC's US Editor), got fed up not getting pieces on the news bulletins.'

From the point of view of the EU Commission, this is seriously damaging. There isn't much it can do. Most of the rebuttals would sound more boring and technical than the original stories themselves, while the exhilarating articles written by tabloids would remain in people's minds. EU institutions also rarely resort to the UK's Press Complaints Commission, or to any other centre for press complaints. They have instead created a website – 'Euromyths'[3] – where a diligent EU official takes the time to reply to the stories run by the British and other media which are regarded as the most inaccurate.

This is exhilarating reading: the list of the 'Euromyths' include the alleged banning of cheese and yogurt from school dinners, cancer drugs for children, sugar banned from jam (to name some recent ones): the site treats these less with indignation, rather resorting to irony. The public relations people, speaking on grounds of anonymity, maintain that it is far more useful to focus on the positive message of what the EU brings to citizens than waste time on negative stories which are so entrenched in the journalistic culture of a country.

George Parker agrees that the issue is not so much with the Euromyths but rather with the rest of the coverage. 'British journalists should be more aware of what goes on in other EU capitals' and tell their readers that 'it is a much more interesting and complicated debate than they thought', he says. But the absence of correspondents from highly critical news organisations is not only a British phenomenon: Matthias Krupa of Germany's *Die Zeit* points out that *Bild* – a tabloid which has, arguably, a greater degree of influence on the German political class, especially over EU issues, than do the British tabloids – also has no permanent correspondent resident in Brussels (we tried to talk to Bild on this, but calls and messages were not returned). '*Bild* gave the worst picture of the Greeks. I would not say that without them [the anti-Greek feeling in Germany] would not have happened, but they did a lot to speed it up', he says, pointing out that 'if you take the Greek issue you wonder whether it was a European problem or a Germany–Greece problem'. Other institutions which are often criticised by Eurosceptics in every country are seldom covered, says Krupa: 'For example the EU Courts of justice are often neglected.'

Jochen Buchsteiner, of the *Frankfurter Allgemeine Zeitung*, says that *Bild* has mounted 'the harshest campaigns' – the tabloid recently stated in its headlines that 'Greeks are twice as rich as Germans' – but they express the 'national sentiment' and the frustration of German people. In his view, 'when you give a lot of money in guarantees and you get back pictures of Merkel with a Hitler moustache, you feel it is not worth the effort'. Such a simplification of reality is likely to raise strong feelings among the readers – the circulation of the paper is an impressive 3.2 million, the largest in Europe. *Bild* is part of the Springer group, 'where you have to sign up for principles when you work with them: always support the Jewish state [Israel], transatlantic relations and the German Constitution', says Buchsteiner.

But much of the narrative about the EU is centred on a model which compares country A with country B, and which is prone to distortion. The Greece vs. Germany case is a good example, a large trope in *Bild*. In the course of the battle between the German and the Greek press, Greeks were advised to sell the Parthenon to pay for their debts and Germans were compared to Nazis. While British tabloids rarely resort to comparisons – the fiend for them is mainly centralised bureaucracy – other media in the EU make a wide use of parallels between their country and another as a shortcut to talk about European affairs. Before the crisis,

Italian and Spanish national media were constantly comparing themselves with the other country, over which was getting richer, which was more socially advanced, which was doing better in general. The stronger and more widely diffused Euroscepticism which has gained ground in the last few years is very often fuelled by a comparative approach: countries tend to compare themselves to Germany or to Northern countries where austerity has not been necessary, while the pejorative acronym of PIIGS – Portugal, Ireland, Italy, Greece, and Spain – has been more influential than expected in creating a wide South–North divide.

In its quest for a more simplistic and enticing language, one which could appeal to a wider readership and thus stop the ongoing sales haemorrhage, the media sector is more and more embracing, not so much Euroscepticism – since that has come to imply a demand for withdrawal from the Union – as increasingly sharp Euro-criticism. News organisations which have been wholly supportive in the past – in Germany, Italy, France, and elsewhere – now take a harder line, pushed into it as much by the public for which they write or broadcast as by their owners. In Italy, the main papers of the right – *Il Giornale* (owned by the Berlusconi family) and *Libero* – have taken an increasingly harsh line on the EU, particularly on German Chancellor Angela Merkel, following the Greek media in labelling her a Nazi. Among the former Comecon states, both Hungary and the Czech Republic have several newspapers, and news channels, which are heavily sceptical. In France, the big newspapers remain pro-European, notwithstanding the large success in the polls of the anti-EU movement led by Marine Le Pen – though the main paper of the centre right, *Le Figaro*, is now more critical.

Tabloids are willing to use nationalist feelings and prejudices, but do not necessarily advocate an exit of their country from the EU. Says Krupa: 'If you put it to *Bild*: would you be for or against the union? then *Bild* is for the union. They of course complain about Greece and the euro; but this was also in the press in the 1990s, when there were many questions about – was it right to give up the D mark? These discussions have come back with a vengeance.' In Germany the party asking for a withdrawal from the eurozone is the quite sophisticated Alternative für Deutschland, whose positions are argued in detailed and often technical language, appropriate for an organisation dominated – at least among its founding members – by economists. Even the British tabloids have so far stopped short of demanding an exit from the EU – though if there is to be a referendum on the issue after the next British general election, one or more of them may decide that the game should be up.

9

The Globalists: Reporting for the Elite

We don't have a home country.

(Paul Taylor, Reuters)

The creation and sustaining of the European Union has been from the beginning, and remains, an elite endeavour: it was undertaken by a group of intellectuals and senior politicians, called into being not to address this or that social issue but for a much higher purpose. It was designed to end European war: and the moral force of that gave the project wide support. Uniting as it did from the outset three large European states – France, Germany, and Italy – together with Belgium, Luxembourg, and the Netherlands, the Union saw off the challenge from the British-sponsored (and much less politically ambitious) European Free Trade Area and drew to it countries like Spain and Greece, emerging from authoritarian rule; three of the Scandinavian states – Denmark, Finland, and Sweden; the former Comecon states after the collapse of communism in Eastern Europe; and even the UK.

The great successes of the Union in expanding to, and especially in providing support for, relatively poor countries emerging from communism as well as those sloughing off dictatorship, masked a central problem. That is, the element of participative democracy was inevitably low. Inevitably, since the EU was in search of 'ever closer union' – a goal which could only be reached when the Union became a state, or at least took on most of the appurtenances of a state. As the crisis has shown, a common currency would have required common basic fiscal, banking, and tax arrangements to be stable: if – as many politicians and officials say they wish – these are put in place, then political institutions must be developed to act as a democratic correlative, the development exerting a ratchet effect which would see power flowing to the European centre, away from the national governments and parliaments. While this process continues, the putative centre cannot find democratic legitimacy, while the national centres lose it.

The French liberal political philosopher Pierre Manent describes this period as a perilous one – where an old form is being discredited and a new one not constructed or even properly envisaged by the large majority of Europeans. 'During the twentieth century, the nation-state was discredited and is now increasingly regarded as a type of human association that belongs to a past age,' he writes. The new political form which has been envisaged is Europe, 'a Europe that already constitutes a part of their experience, though in an extremely limited and artificial way'. The philosopher believes Europeans find themselves 'at a point of transition from one type of human association to another – and they will not be governed well until they face the question that is once again thrust upon them: the question of political form'.[1] This transition became less comfortable because of the crisis, which made a vast portion of EU citizens uneasy about some of the consequences of the EU project.

As we've noted, most news media need a nation: and thus they too are caught, when covering Europe, in a trough between the leeching away of the power of their main subjects (their government and state) and the unknown quality which is a future United States of Europe. We've also noted, however, that a handful of newspapers – *The Economist*, the *Financial Times*, the *Wall Street Journal*, and to a less engaged extent the *International New York Times* – together with the global news services, the Euronews channel and (insofar as they cover European Union matters) the global broadcasters such as BBC World, CNN, Deutsche Welle, and France 24, occupy a particular niche of esteem in Brussels. They occupy that niche because of the detail in their reporting and the relatively large resources they bring to bear; and they can do so because they have a global 'nation': a transnational elite of business people, senior officials, politicians, diplomats, policy strategists, scholars, and NGOs – the 'Davos people', either in fact or in aspiration.

The articles written for the *Financial Times*, the *Wall Street Journal,* or *The Economist* are often more complex than those published elsewhere, and usually more numerous: they are also distinguished by the fact that they strive to have no national angle, and carry little of the 'what is the EU doing for my country?' material common elsewhere. Reporting the EU as if it were a domestic story is seen by most Brussels reporters as inevitable because 'there is no European public, there is a European elite', according to Hughes Beaudouin of LC1/TF1. When the EU was awarded the Nobel

Prize for peace in October 2012, 'the elite rejoiced, but people were in tears,' he says. In France the main reaction was 'to laugh'.

Even though at its peak the debt crisis harmonised the media coverage in different member states, evidence suggests that the European dimension of journalism is not yet developed, while elite journalism has been developing for some years now.[2] Thus when Peter Spiegel, the *FT* Brussels bureau chief, notes that most of his colleagues largely write about what Europe does or doesn't do for their countries, he is implicitly commenting on their still-developing economic tragedy. His newspaper is, presently, one of the few islands relatively safe from a wave of cuts, closures, and desperate manoeuvres to stay alive. He is able to write about the EU as 'Europe' for a European, indeed an international, audience which is more concerned with the transnational than the national, at least in their working lives. The same holds true for Anton La Guardia of *The Economist* – 'I see things from Brussels. The story must be about a project as a whole and a reader in Poland has to be interested in what I am writing about France.' Spiegel says his editor pitched the Brussels job to him by saying: 'You must do this as a story for the world, not just as a story to Europe.'

German newspapers tried to have a different approach. 'What we do here is between foreign correspondent and domestic news. You would not cover a foreign country like this', says Matthias Krupa. Jochen Buchsteiner, based in London, says that the German attitude is one of taking a deliberately low profile – because of the country's power. It's an attitude which encourages a loftier, and broader, view of Europe: but which in the end comes back, also, to what he sees as a national imperative: the need to avoid a display of arrogance, to 'protect the Germans from themselves', as Buchsteiner puts it. '*Zurückhaltung* is the word that best describes German attitude. It means restraint. We don't want to be isolated in Europe ever again. It is very important to be close to someone', he says. Ruth Berschens of *Handelsblatt* believes that German impartiality is mainly due to sheer numbers: 'There are good journalists from all countries. The difference for the Germans is that they are more wealthy, have more resources, and more people.'

Besides the global papers, the big news agencies – Reuters, Bloomberg, AP, AFP – strive for what Paul Taylor calls 'a neutral or Martian perspective': that is, a conscious and constant effort to tell the story as if from nowhere. No news, of course, can be from nowhere: one of the ways in which Reuters strives for a greater objectivity than others is to have a bureau in which a number of different nationalities are represented by the reporters – 'so that with a French and a German correspondent, it was very helpful, we could tap into some of the emotion in the national debates which corrected what might have been a bias'. Taylor uses an effective image: 'We don't have a home country'. In terms of sourcing this means relying 'a lot on the little countries which don't have as many dogs in the fights to tell it straight – like the Nordic countries, for example, which have an admirable tradition of open government'. Avoiding national government spin is crucial, for this type of medium: 'The Brits and the Germans and others will, when they're engaged in a big negotiation, naturally give their side of it.'

10

Dog Does Eat Dog: Peer Pressure and Peer Reviews

> I don't say my colleagues here know nothing, but they lack depth. That's the central problem. There's a loss of substance.
>
> (Jean Quatremer, *Libération*)

As they often comment, the members of the Brussels press corps live in a small community, clustered around the main institutions of the EU in the centre of Brussels. They display some of the camaraderie which groups of journalists usually do – though languages can be a barrier and the correspondents are not immune from viewing their colleagues through the prism of national stereotypes. What they think of each other professionally at times betrays these stereotypes – but also illuminates the way in which they think journalism should be done.

Enrico Tibuzzi of the Italian news service ANSA – who believes that journalists should be open about their opinions for or against the EU – says that 'there is not a sense of a mutual cause among journalists. There is a tendency to limit the reporting to the perspectives of the country. The press room is not more integrated, not at all. Even the *FT* represents specific interests quite often.' His fellow countryman David Carretta of *Il Foglio*, however, thinks that the *Financial Times*, *Les Échos*, and the *Wall Street Journal* 'are doing great work, and it's not propaganda. In Italy the Il Sole-24 Ore coverage is quite correct and objective, but they do have a soft spot for [Euro] propaganda.'

He is scathing, however, about most of his colleagues' reporting – saying that 'reporters here should have an objective role, namely to report in a clear way what happens and then to find an interpretation to it'. In his view 'many Italian media are absolutely superficial in the way they cover the news, without understanding that they influence the political class'.

Noting how a widespread use of foreign newswires, sometimes bad translations of newswires, has 'an impact on the decision-making on a political level and among opinion-makers', he suggests this might be the result of an existing 'pattern and project', namely the creation of 'the perfect scapegoat to all internal problems inside member states'. There could be a political reason not to fix issues concerning the reporting of such a sensitive issue: 'Editors are chosen by the paper's ownership, and owners are not always only publishers, but quite often key actors of the national political life.'

Observers coming from several member states point out, echoing Carretta, that a crucial topic like the debt crisis has been 'reported as if it was just a football match, with fights between countries'. The amateurism 'concerning economics and finance', in particular, is due to the lack of background, of a summary of what happened previously, of instruments to help viewers understand what was going on. The frustration with the lack of understanding paved the way to scepticism towards the EU as it was seen as a remote and distant entity: scepticism is a by-product of the lack of clarity. 'I appreciate the British papers and I sometimes think that Eurosceptic editorials are often more interesting. They surely are more entertaining. At least when the *Telegraph* says something, you know what it stands for', he points out. 'In Italy journalists are entitled to say whatever they want without specifying what they stand for.'

Criticising the media of one's own country is popular in Brussels – perhaps because it shows that the speaker is not tied to a my-country-right-or-wrong point of view, perhaps because these are the media one knows best. Toby Vogel writes for one of the best-known of the specialist publications aimed at EU insiders – *European Voice*. Founded by the Economist Group in 1995, it was sold in 2013 to the French company Selectcom, whose goal is to 'increase *European Voice*'s influence, circulation and readership, taking it beyond Brussels and the European Union's leaders to reach decision-makers and key influencers in the national capitals', according to the press release published on the acquisition. 'We are perceived as a British media, but we are also rabidly pro-European by British standards', points out Vogel. In his view there is a stigma in taking the EU seriously among British media.

Philippe Ricard of *Le Monde* conveys a long-held view about the English-language or Anglo-Saxon media – that they are too much in thrall to the markets:

> *the crisis has not only been economic, and when it became too economic,*
> *we tried to put it back on other pages, to see other sides of the story. I*
> *refuse to remain prisoner of the markets. The Anglo-Saxon press has not*
> *seen the political power. It has been chaotic and we had to ask the Germans*
> *to move, but the most intense and difficult part was the political one.*

Krupa of *Die Zeit* also sees the Anglo-Saxon influence as strong:
though he does not define it, it's clear he sees it as one which endorses
liberal economics (the customary phrase, usually derogatory, is
'neo-liberal'):

> *if I look at the ideological trend in the FT – how they comment on the euro*
> *crisis – there is a very clear Anglo-Saxon perspective. We are not free from*
> *the perspectives of the countries we come from. A bit less in The Economist.*
> *But if The Economist gives a recommendation before the German*
> *elections – they would vote for the [economically liberal] Free Democratic*
> *Party continuing in the [Christian Democratic/Christian Social Union*
> *dominated] coalition – they were probably the only one which did so.*

Bettina Schulz was the financial correspondent of the *FAZ* in
London. Her 20-year-long career in the German paper came to an end
because of her divergence of views with the editor of the economic
section, Holger Steltzner: the story ended bitterly, in court. Buchsteiner
has pointed out that 'the economic section is not critical of the German
approach' and suggested that Steltzner has a position very close to the
one of Alternative für Deutschland, the anti-euro party. *FAZ* has five
editors, one for each section, and decisions are taken collegially, but the
stance on the EU, for example, is not the same in every section: the
political one is more pro-integration, while the economic section is
increasingly sceptical.

According to Schulz, much of the German press is affected by the
'massive interference of the Bundesbank', and in particular of its president,
Jens Weidmann, whose stance, during the crisis, emerged as the most
'hawkish' and fiercely pro-austerity in the whole European press. This is
particularly true of the *FAZ*, where the economic pages are 'driven by a
very rigid theoretical economic view', influenced by economists like Otmar
Issing, former chief economist of the ECB, Hans-Werner Sinn, president of
the IFO institute for economic research, and Thilo Sarrazin, a right-wing
economist and former member of the Bundesbank whose book on the

failed integration of Turks and Arabs into Germany in 2010 sold a million copies[1] – as did, a couple of years later, his *Europe Doesn't Need the Euro*.[2]

Schulz's troubles started when she did not agree with the German orthodox economic view that Greece needed only austerity in order to recover. 'On the Greek crisis I could write only other people's opinion', she says. The German approach to recovery, heavily criticised by many economists across the EU and the world, was based on the idea that Greeks and other 'profligate' countries had to pay for their own mistakes through expense cuts and other austerity measures.

Reporting from the City of London, Schulz was of course exposed to different opinions coming from bankers and the financial environment. In a time of paralysis and deep crisis like that of the summer of 2012, the City view of the insecurity of the ECB's mandate was one of the main issues. The Bundesbank president famously opposed the measures of the European Central Bank president, Mario Draghi, who announced the buying of bonds of distressed countries if they adhered to a rescue programme in order to ease the pressure. 'When Merkel said the ECB was acting within its mandate it was very important because she was giving her support to Draghi, notwithstanding the fierce opposition of the Bundesbank', says Schulz. When she tried to report the sense of relief with which the City welcomed the announcement of the ECB, her pitch was ignored. She was then offered relocation to Frankfurt for what were said to be economic reasons: she, however, took the newspaper to court, lost, and decided not to appeal, but negotiate a settlement and leave.

The outstanding feature of Bettina Schulz's story is that it summarises many of the aspects of the debate of the economic crisis. It shows how positions became polarised on both sides, and how the euro crisis became a battle between two different German factions, who found one of their battlefields in the news media. 'I was not writing an opinion piece, it was just a fact-based article', she claims. On the German press in general, Schulz points out that 'German journalists look too much at the German economy and have little understanding of the periphery.' In the hall of mirrors that is the European Union, it is easy to find scapegoats to avoid the truth and build a narrative on them: bankers were the scapegoats for the financial crisis, Southern Europeans were those for the economic crisis, according to Schulz. Her views, deemed unorthodox in some German circles, have been very widespread elsewhere in the EU.[3]

A good example of this is when the US pointed out that Germany's trade surplus was too high and that its internal demand was too weak.

The IMF agreed and many others voiced their concern about a situation which, in their view, hampered the economic recovery of the eurozone, damaging weaker countries. Germany defined the US Treasury report 'incomprehensible' and the *FAZ*'s Philip Plickert wrote that the surplus was a 'consequence of the structural strength of the domestic economy, which is not a problem'. The clash between Southern and Nordic countries is one of the fractures which will be harder to heal over time and Bettina Schulz's case shows how the reporting about the EU is as much influenced as influential. For Buchsteiner, 'the aim of enlarging and deepening the Union at the same time was a contradiction which is becoming more and more obvious. I don't think that a referendum for federal Europe would have very good results.'

Chris Morris of the BBC makes a general point of many of his colleagues:

> my impression is that too many journalists write or broadcast in the language of the bubble – terminology which no one knows, committees no one has ever heard of. And though it's often very hostile, much of what is written isn't very incisive. It's been churned out for the sake of churning out. A Reuters Institute survey showed that 80% of the coverage was on financial economic news, 20% only on social and political. You do have a specialist audience, but the esoteric stuff became the mainstream story – and tended to be lost.

The correspondent prepared to be most expansive about his colleagues was Peter Spiegel of the *Financial Times* – perhaps because, as an American, he feels himself (as he said) a little to one side of an overwhelmingly European corps. And though he is critical of what he sees as the chauvinism of the coverage, he makes a general point which others also made: that is, that the problem lies as much with the audience (or lack of it) as with the journalists. 'If you look for it there's plenty of excellent coverage of the EU', he says, mentioning German media, the *WSJ*, and Reuters as positive examples. The problem, in his view, is that 'people don't want coverage', they will not buy a newspaper because of its European coverage. It was the case at the peak of the crisis, but it is not happening any more. 'Is it the journalists' fault that the stuff isn't read – or the consumers'?' he asks.

Spiegel praises his most direct competitor – 'the *Wall Street Journal* has got a lot better. It didn't take the EU very seriously, now it does.' He adds, however, that 'the problem is no one reads them. The *Journal* claimed a 75,000 circulation in the EU. But half of that was paid by them – they lent money to a Dutch company which bought half the run. The *Guardian* broke the story – then to their credit the *Journal* did it too, even tougher. So the number of people who have fully paid up copies – 5,000 only.'[4]

The Economist's La Guardia says that 'the most complete coverage would be the *FT*. The *Journal* has slightly deeper reporting – more explanation, but doesn't break as many stories. You must read Quatremer, you must read *Le Monde*. You should read German pieces.' Brussels is the source of a myriad of different sorts of information, and the only serious 'problem is interpreting it and making sense of it'.

Like Spiegel, Quatremer is generous with the number of comments about his colleagues, though less generous about his colleagues – 'I think the coverage here in Brussels is too technocratic. To cover the financial crisis without covering the effects of the crisis on the ground is bizarre.' In his view experience is crucial when reporting from Brussels in order to have a wide-ranging perspective.

'I don't say my colleagues here know nothing, but they lack depth', he says, talking about a 'loss of substance', in part, he believes, due to the fact that some British and American journalists speak only English. 'You're confined to the official sources. But what about the conversations in the salons, in the corridors – that's where you get the news.' Quatremer, however, is arguably more challenged: he speaks little English, now the official language of the EU and the one which most commissioners and officials speak well, as (if not their first) their second language. Says Quatremer: 'I was going to learn English, but my father said – you must learn German. Why? He said: because they may return.'

Quatremer, prone to overkill in his judgements, makes a serious point when he says:

> One of the problems is the eternal problem of journalism, which is to inflate the story – and that's got much worse. If you read the papers and believed them you'd kill yourself, they say of that which went well – really, that's bad. And if it is bad, it's worse. In 1992 and 1993 there was also an economic crash, now forgotten, especially in the UK – and it was the end of the world, a disaster – the catastrophism is one of the biggest problems. I never say in my pieces – it's the end. If you say that all the time, how could you describe Europe in the 1940s? How could you find words?

11

Tweeting into Clarity: Online is Demanding, But Helpful

> Twitter has been fantastic for the finance crisis ... Ironically the more difficult the subject, the more useful Twitter was.
>
> (Chris Morris, BBC)

Many of the correspondents we spoke to blog, but since most serve conventional media outlets, it is a minor part of their work, and sometimes one to which they do not give a great deal of attention. La Guardia of *The Economist* says that 'I do the Charlemagne column – I do the blog, I tweet; rarely do news. My first, second and third priority is the column. That's what people here read. The blog has changed – it was tied to me, now it's a European blog. You do lose the personal voice. I blog less but tweet more.' Charlemagne is a must-read in Brussels: *The Economist's* former Brussels correspondent David Rennie brought it to its current levels.

Tweeting, by contrast, has been the real aid to embattled correspondents seeking explanations to complexities with whose details they are unfamiliar. Chris Morris says that

> *Twitter has been fantastic for the finance crisis. You can do things like follow hedge fund managers whom I normally wouldn't speak to in the course of my daily work – and as a resource for finding instant informed analysis on crucial issues it's wonderful.*
>
> *Like everything on Twitter it's all about finding the right people to follow. Ironically the more difficult the subject the more useful Twitter was. If you find the right people you have sources with rare expertise – they're putting stuff out for free – before, their companies would have charged thousands for that. There's quite a lot of 140-character analysis but there's also linking to other stuff – so it's a short cut to detailed information, which might have taken you hours to find.*

Spiegel – encouraged by his newspaper, which is rapidly shifting on to the web – both tweets and blogs.

> *Tweets are not very time consuming – blogging is more. But I like the discipline. If I have read the entire IMF report on the Greek bailout, I'll write it at 400 words for the paper, but then I will do a blog on interesting detailed facets of it – for example, direct the reader to the chart on page x. I don't subscribe to the argument that because we are so inundated with multimedia we have no time to do the real job. In the old days – how much time did I spend kibitzing [gossiping]? It's time management. Also I don't believe too much in investigative reporting – they often don't have an impact. The real impact is that which takes you a week or two. See the National Security Agency [Snowden leaks] story – it was traditional reporting – a Washington Post guy with sources. But it's hard if you are a one person bureau. You can't do everything. I have the possibility to go off the diary, since there are four of us.*
>
> *Social media have changed coverage a lot – especially Twitter. I had no economic background. On Twitter you have a lot of very active bond traders – and so you can see in real time how reactions are going in the market and it did shape my coverage. I rely on it a lot. I have 20,000 followers. So – we get a leaked document and I put it on the blog. I will tweet that an official says something and a full analysis comes later. And being on Twitter helps in other ways. I was in Berlin, wanted to meet the economics people in the SPD – we called up the man I wanted to meet, and he says Peter Spiegel! I follow him on Twitter! I'd love to meet him! So it's good from a sourcing dimension. But also from a profiling point of view.*

Jean Quatremer uses his blog to speak to fellow insiders – a form of writing which allows him to deploy his contacts and experience, and to escape the need for simplification. He says that

> *I have two publics. For Libération, it's French. For the blog, it's Europe. The thing is, you have to explain all the time – because the technocratic vocabulary isn't understood and you have to explain and then explain again. It's like a financial vocabulary. The EU remains something outside of their experience; it's a small elite who can master it. Yesterday I talked to a group of young socialists – very pro-European; and one of them said – isn't the problem that the EU has no power. I said – what, no*

power? And had to explain the powers it has. (See Appendix 2 for an example of Quatremer's blog.)

This use of the blog points to one of the firmer developments in the confused present state of journalism. Increasingly, online journalism is successful (though rarely makes a profit) where it targets specific groups, and becomes part of, or organises, their professional conversations. Such groups are best for interaction: online journalism comes into its own when the journalist is in constant dialogue with readers and followers who are equally or more involved in the issues covered than the journalist themselves.

The European Commission, and the European Parliament, along with other EU institutions, have a familiar and well-presented presence on the web. It's useful to reporters as well as to the general public: but Hughes Baudouin injects a sour note on it – noting that 'before [the web] there was the possibility of getting a lot in the off-record time – now everything goes out on the Web anyway, and there's no off the record'. It's a further instance of the pressure now being exerted on mainstream media: for every gain, to the public, there's a pain to the journalists, as they are deprived of the gates they used to keep.

The flash of resentment that the Commission and other institutions should now be promoting technologies which allow easier public access to information on their activities reflects a reluctance of the mainstream media to radically reassess the way in which they work – though reporters, who tend to be conservative, are being pushed to change by their managements, who realise more clearly that economic viability depends on it (even if change cannot guarantee a return to profitability). Reporters in Brussels blog and tweet: however, a reassessment of how far their reporting could benefit from the kind of collaborative reporting adumbrated in Columbia Journalism School's *Post Industrial Journalism*[1] – bringing in other players, including the public – appears to be at best in the early stages. Yet it seems that the small, intense, highly specialised world of Brussels politics and media would seem to lend itself to some such experiment – with the public beyond the usual EU circles brought into the coverage.

12

The Next Act: Journalism in a Time of Polemics

> Too many of our media miss the commonalities of stories across Europe and thus miss much of the story.
>
> (Bill Emmott, former editor, *The Economist*)

What about the public?

The journalism on the European Union is rich, varied, detailed, and combative: the crisis showed its deficiencies but also sharpened and broadened its practice. The largest challenge – that of conveying something of its reality and its importance for good or ill to a wider audience – remains, in most member states, only partially met.

First, TV as the dominant news medium has striven to make the subject more interesting. The structural problems are formidable: but more should be attempted. That might include:

- Trying to make the substantive work of the EU more interesting, by constructing stories out of the large issues with which its institutions have to deal – such as unemployment, lagging educational standards, and the effects of immigration.
- Giving more visibility to the Parliament and to its multiple voices, now more easily done because of higher profile and fundamentalist opposition forces.
- Increasing the coverage of other EU countries through more varied current affairs programmes and documentaries on different European states, highlighting their politics, economic state, and above all their cultures, with a strong emphasis on popular culture. These should also include debates and documentaries taking a frank and honest

approach, one in which the defects are highlighted just as much as the qualities.

Second, the EU's press spokespersons are, even their critics admit, often expert in the fields whose brief they have. The constraints under which they operate – that they have multiple 'masters' in the member states of the EU who are alert to deviations from what they see as agreed positions – makes the job inevitably more constraining than a spokesman or woman for a cabinet minister of a national state.

However, there should be a renewed effort on the part of the EU's public relations machines to engage the mass-circulation newspapers and magazines in the main issues of the EU institutions and policies. Insofar as they have developed a defensive, even hostile, stance against what they see as the aggression of journalists and some news organisations, this should be replaced by a continuing attempt to reach out and discuss the activities of the EU without resorting to strongly normative messages, absorbing and debating criticism rather than regarding it as ill intentioned, even where it is.

This will be particularly important in the future, as the political debate within the Parliament and thus within the other institutions of the Union become more polarised. The press service must resist the temptation to be an arm of the 'pro-Union-ists' ranged against the 'anti-Union-ists'. That would be to increase polarisation.

Third, no journalism about complex processes can itself avoid complexity. To grasp the main lines of development of contemporary society and politics one must learn how to learn: which means education in both contemporary civics and in how to approach and learn from journalism, which can be taught in both schools and colleges. This has wider application than to the EU: but lack of knowledge of it, and the bases on which it can be either opposed or supported, is among the more notable gaps in the understanding of contemporary centres of power.

The lack of comprehension of the EU is one of the clearest arguments for the teaching of current affairs literacy at school and colleges: to assume that a public largely ignorant of the main pillars of their public life can properly orient themselves is increasingly a luxury. The European Union, its history, and institutions would be part of such a project.

However, such teaching on the workings of the EU should avoid the situation reportedly common with the Jean Monnet chairs in European universities: that they can become centres for conveying the inevitability of increasing integration. 'More Europe' in education about the European Union is an inappropriate posture.

Fourth, the EU project is mature enough for journalists to learn the lessons from the crisis and start holding the Commission and the EU institutions much more to account. The crisis has shown that a skilled and usually hard-working news media corps have been able to upgrade their knowledge and understanding, and in many case give good coverage of complex issues.

There is no longer any excuse – if there ever was – for obscure reporting or jargon about the EU. The press has power both with its readership and with its sources. The EU can only improve if journalists start making their point clear.

The fact that Europe is increasingly covered by other desks than the foreign department is a good sign, unless it is exclusively covered by them (that is, with no correspondent based in Brussels or at least often there). Teamwork between Brussels and local desks has to be increased.

Covering the EU has to become something wider than covering Brussels. The crisis has shown that important – often more important – events happen in different capitals. As Bill Emmott noted, in a talk at Johns Hopkins University's School of Advanced International Studies in Bologna in February 2014, a chance is usually missed to use Brussels as the centre of a journalism which compares European experiences and makes the comparisons into compelling stories.

Emmott, himself a former Brussels correspondent, believes that broad cross-European stories are largely uncovered: these include the fall in productivity relative to other major economies; the decline of Europe's schools and universities; the increase in unemployment and the sluggishness of growth; the continuing neglect of the issues of climate change; the job-destroying effects of automation – the 'race against the machine'; the burden of sovereign debt, still rising in countries like Italy; fears of further future weakness in Europe's geopolitical status in the world; an apparent weakening of scientific and other innovation, as the numbers of Nobel Prizes decrease – and much else.

These issues make up an agenda for the news media – one which stands behind the day-by-day events and announcements, and which gives meaning to the more open arguments likely to come in the Parliament, and the closed-door debates among officials, commissioners, and national politicians in the Commission.

Appendix 1

Euroscepticism: Boris Johnson and Bruno Waterfield

The British still command the heights of Euroscepticism. It's strong in varying degrees in the *Daily Mail* and *Mail on Sunday*; in the *Sun* and the *Sun on Sunday*; in *The Times* and the *Sunday Times*; in the *Daily Star* and the *Daily Star Sunday*; in the *Daily Express* and *Sunday Express*; in the *Daily Telegraph* and the *Sunday Telegraph*. Those which are to a greater or lesser degree supportive of the EU are the Mirror group papers (*Daily Mirror*, *Sunday Mirror*, and *Sunday People*); the *Independent* and *Independent on Sunday*; the *Guardian* and the *Observer*; and the *Financial Times*. By circulation – a less useful measure in the internet age – Eurosceptic papers represent more than two-thirds of newspaper circulation.

The Eurosceptic papers differ: what is meant by labelling them Eurosceptic is that they concentrate, in news and above all in comment, on the downsides of the EU, and support national as against European governance. None, so far, has come out unambiguously for an exit from the EU. It's commonly thought in Continental Europe that the UK public opinion is for leaving the Union: in fact, as this is written in spring 2014, YouGov polls show a small majority in favour of staying in, after some time in which a small majority of those polled wanted out. The press, like the public at large, haven't decided yet.

We illuminate British Euroscepticism through the two correspondents of the *Telegraph*, Boris Johnson, presently Mayor of London; and Bruno Waterfield, who has been the *Telegraph*'s Brussels correspondent for eight years.

Johnson's career there, much loved by those who dislike the EU and by those who have no opinion on it but like fun, is a vivid case of Anglo-Saxon Europhobia – made the more entertaining and intriguing for having a postmodern edge to it, as if Johnson's reporting knew it was both over the top and frequently factually wrong, but was putting the whole thing in invisible quotes.

Johnson, at the age of 25, had a lucky break – he was hired by the then *Daily Telegraph* editor Max Hastings, who employed him, after an uninspiring short stint at *The Times*, as a lead writer, then after a year sent him, in 1989, to Brussels as the EU correspondent. In his *Boris* (from where much of this material on him is taken),[1] his admiring and lively biographer Andrew Gimson writes that 'his stories on the idiocies of the European Union were received with rapture by an ever-growing circle of fans [...] his work was so marvelously enjoyable because he debunked an institution which almost everyone else reporting from Brussels was still treating with reverence'.

Johnson's debunking was, in the eyes of other colleagues, just wrong. Rory Watson, who wrote for the now defunct *European*, said that 'He made stories up'. David Usborne, who covered the EU for the *Independent*, said that 'he was fundamentally intellectually dishonest ... I never felt he believed a word ... he really began to eclipse all of us. He was having fun.'

Sarah Helm, the *Independent*'s diplomatic correspondent, said that she remembers 'developing an instinctive feel that Boris was a complete charlatan ... it [his writing] was a cheap thrill – a stunt and quite a dangerous one really'. George Parker of the *FT*, in Brussels in the 2000s sometime after Johnson's period, believes by contrast that 'some of the best journalism ever committed in Brussels is from a still-vilified person, the Mayor of London Boris Johnson. His stories were beautifully reported.'

Gimson recounts, in *Boris*, that Johnson took the story that the Commission was considering leaving the Berlaymont building because it was leaking asbestos – and turned it into an epic, suggesting that the building would be blown up. His story on the 'Delors Plan to Rule Europe' helped make him Prime Minister Margaret Thatcher's favourite journalist – since she too believed that was Delors's aim (the report was not wholly fanciful: Delors did see 'ever closer union', and thus more power to the European Union centre, as his overriding goal).

Alan Phelps was a long-time correspondent for the *Daily Telegraph* and Foreign Editor in the early 2000s: his rigorous reporting style was quite unlike the man who was EU correspondent while he was in Moscow, but he's indulgent about it.

> *Boris was sent there to shake things up and he did. Journalists usually like to be trouble makers. There is a certain amount of willingness to stretch*

the truth to get a good story. No paper doesn't like bad news – it's what makes it news. Apart from the pro-EU papers like the FT, the Guardian and the Independent, they're looking for stories which will reflect badly on the EU.

Waterfield, correspondent since 2006, is more interesting because he is a genuine – rather than a playful – Eurosceptic; and though his reports contain exaggeration, they also use exaggeration to make serious points. When asked if he uses his reporting as an expression of his beliefs, he responds that

you must have the facts – you must be right about the who, when, where, what, why. I also do see part of my job as being part of the public debate, and taking the consequences of that.

But I make a distinction between my reporting and my position [anti-EU]. My reputation as a journalist is important to me. Boris was different – he was already an associate editor when here. He was a Conservative – ambitious for something other than journalism.

No journalist is entirely immune from the national interest and appeals to it. A British journalist isn't, any more than the rest. The cultural shift in France [from enthusiasm to a more sceptical stance] is very important: it did change their attitude. France has always been quite conscious of the national interest, and of the overlap between the national and the European interest.

Waterfield, more than any other journalist we spoke to, is acutely conscious of the pull of nationalism and patriotism, the sense that people are fully French, or German, or Dutch, and could be nothing else. It leads him to listen to others whom his colleagues might simply automatically revile with greater interest:

I have listened to Le Pen in the French parliament several times – she advances what is in part a left Gaullist, even socialist position – the need for the collective to be coterminous with the territory. So in the eurozone – the budgetary constraints now dictate how the French will spend their national wealth. Yet most people would say that my first loyalty is to my own.

The finance ministers are only now grappling with the implications of what they have done. If you're a social democrat it would come hard on you. Some French socialists have said that the fiscal pact makes a French socialist programme impossible.

Waterfield ended the interview by referring us to the last paragraph of the late Tony Judt's massive *Postwar: A History of Europe since 1945*.[2] Judt ends the book by writing that

> *the new Europe, bound together by the signs and symbols of its terrible past, is a remarkable accomplishment; but it remains forever mortgaged to that past. If Europeans are to maintain this vital link – if Europe's past is to continue to furnish Europe's present with admonitory meaning and more purpose – then it will have to be taught afresh with every passing generation. 'European Union' may be a response to history, but it can not be a substitute.*

An example of the style

A story by Waterfield for the *Telegraph* – 'Leveson: EU wants power to sack journalists'[3] – was published on 22 January 2013. The piece was based on a just-published report, *A Free and Pluralistic Media to Sustain European Democracy*, written by a 'High level group on media freedom and pluralism'.[4]

Their report of some 40 pages was replete with calls for freedom and pluralism of the media to be both respected and protected. Waterfield's report did not mention these.

However, it did focus strongly on one recommendation, which was to propose that all EU member states should have independent media councils with the power to impose fines, order print or broadcast apologies, and 'remove journalistic status' – these to be monitored by the Commission 'to ensure that they comply with European values'. It also quoted from a brief discussion in the report on the Leveson Inquiry into phone hacking in UK tabloids – the EU report noting that Leveson's recommendations had been 'rejected out of hand by some politicians in high office' which was 'not very reassuring'. In fact, all party leaders endorsed nearly all of Leveson's findings and recommendations: comparatively few criticised them, with only Michael Gove, the then Secretary of State for Education, among cabinet ministers coming out strongly against.

The report did not explicitly say, as the *Telegraph* story claimed it did, that EU officials would be 'given control of national media supervisors' with the power to sack journalists: but the formulation was vague. It did not specify what 'journalistic status' was – a disputed term when millions of bloggers have appeared. It was also vague as to the EU's basis for having oversight of media councils, and on how far this oversight would be enshrined in law. The report, whose recommendations have not to date been acted upon, did have in some passages a bias towards greater control, though these were buttressed by many more clauses supporting freedom and plurality.

The downside of the *Telegraph* report was that it was almost wholly one-sided, giving no space to the recommendations on press freedom. On the other hand, it did powerfully draw attention to an apparent tendency to wish to involve the EU, perhaps on a legal basis, in an area – the press – which in most countries is unregulated by the state.

The Eurosceptic reporting of (mainly) the British is often criticised for its frequent inaccuracy and hyperbole: the website begun by the Commission to set the record straight is normally deployed against the UK tabloids, none of whom have a Brussels correspondent. Much of that reporting is justified under the rubric of 'fun': it may be rubbish, but it makes you laugh, or experience an invigorating spurt of indignation.

The vigour and irreverence of the Eurosceptic reporting did assist, and still does assist, at times in pointing out the emperor's nakedness in a way in which more supportive, even relatively neutral, reporting cannot and has not. Taken with a truth warning – these reports may damage your understanding of what really happened – Eurosceptic reporting has the value which disruptive and unregulated media always have: the occasional ability to hit on the head a nail which more accurate and careful media ignore.

Appendix 2

The Passionate Chronicler: Jean Quatremer

When asked who, in his view, is the most prominent journalist in Brussels, Jean Quatremer simply replies: 'It's me, I am the star.'

In the 24 years he has spent as the Brussels correspondent of the leftist newspaper *Libération*, the French journalist has built a reputation as a committed supporter of the European project but also, surprisingly enough, as one of its most feared critics: his role was crucial in bringing down the Santer Commission in 1999 due to the expenses scandal. The same was true during the 'mad cow' affair, which the EU authorities tried to cover up for a very long time. In recent years his pieces have been just as belligerent; he has, for instance, never concealed his distaste for José Manuel Barroso, the man who has chaired the EU Commission for a decade.

The Anglo-Saxon ideal of journalism based on values like impartiality and objectivity is quite distant from the work of Quatremer who, according to *FT*'s Peter Spiegel, is acting as a 'polemicist' rather than as a journalist. Still, Anton La Guardia of *The Economist* says that the French journalist's articles are a mandatory reading for any person willing to follow European affairs. 'You must read Quatremer,' he says, expressing a very widespread opinion in the EU capital. He is a vehement critic of the 'clubby' EU press room – like Bruno Waterfield of the *Telegraph* (see Appendix 1), who thinks Quatremer is an 'exception, a case apart' among French journalists.

Besides his articles for *Libération*, Quatremer's main activity is his blog, 'Les Coulisses de Bruxelles' (Brussels Offstage) which enjoys a wide readership among EU officials and has become, over the years, as close as one can get to an EU *agora*. As he says: 'I have two publics. For *Libération* it is French, for the blog it is European.' A huge network of relationships in Brussels and elsewhere in Europe helps the *Libération* correspondent to shape his own, fiercely argued interpretation of the stories he finds. He acts as a 'filter', a trusted interpreter of EU's intricacies, and this has so far proved to be one of the most successful approaches in engaging the public on such a technical, confusing, multi-faceted topic.

A recent example of his blog – which uses its author's long patrol of the Brussels corridors and his close observation of the main actors to produce denunciations, character sketches, and waspish insights – is one of 8 March 2014, commenting on the selection of the former Luxembourg premier Jean-Claude Juncker as the centre right's candidate for the post of President of the Commission. Quatremer writes that

> the victory of Jean-Claude Juncker is less decisive than his German supporters hoped; of 812 representatives, 199 didn't vote and two returned blank ballots, giving him a win with 47% of the representatives supporting him (61% of those voting). Even if the European People's Party, dominated head and shoulders by the German CDU/CSU, could not refuse the Chancellor's wishes, it seems that a part of representatives haven't welcomed having themselves represented by one of the dinosaurs of the construction of the European Union. Even if he's only 59, Juncker is actually the last negotiator of the Maastricht Treaty still active [he was then Finance Minister, since 1989].

> Above all, as a member of the European Council of heads of state and government from January 1995 to November 2013 in his role as Prime Minister of the Grand Duchy, and head of the Eurogroup (ministers of finance of the eurozone) between 2004 and 2013, he is the incarnation of an intergovernmental, autocratic and austerity-fixated Europe, that which, according to the parliament, is responsible for the impotence of the Union both internally and on the international level. He has underscored the impression of withdrawal which has surrounded his candidature by refusing to campaign, as if the support of Germany was enough.

> Besides, he has never hidden the fact that he's not interested in the Presidency of the Commission, an exhausting job, but in the presidency of the European Council, of heads of state and government. No one has forgotten that he coveted that job in 2009, when he was never a candidate for the presidency of the Commission. Nicolas Sarkozy, then French President, blocked his progress then, because he believed this bonvivant (too many cigarettes, too much booze) had allied himself a little too much with German thinking, and didn't show himself active enough at the beginning of the crisis in 2007–8. At that time, Merkel supported the French President ...

Quatremer expresses daring points of view, but he bases his reports on a belief in the longevity of the EU project. 'I never write in my pieces – it's the end,' he says, debugging his reporting from one of the leitmotivs of most of the articles on the EU: catastrophism. British tabloids use a 'the end is near' approach to get more readers, while Quatremer does the opposite: given that the EU project is strong enough to stand the pressure of a vocal polemics, he invites people to talk about it, to have their say. 'Our elites know we must stay in the EU and in the eurozone, *faute de mieux*', he says, pointing out how necessary it is to explain how the EU works even among Europhiles.

His approach is coherent within a French tradition, where intellectuals and journalists often get a star-like status and are openly and doggedly opinionated. This might not meet the tastes of some foreign readers, acquainted with a clear-cut separation between facts and opinions, but it proves to be more effective in a country where there are no tabloids and where the coverage of the EU has to constantly struggle to overcome the main obstacle: boredom and lack of interest from the reader. 'The French were pro-European when they thought of it as a big France,' says Quatremer, adding: 'The only difference between them and Marine Le Pen is that she's more rational and she says: get out.' In France the EU constitutional treaty was rejected in a referendum in 2005 and the country is a curious mix of staunch defence of the communitarian project and popular rejection.

In a way, Quatremer managed to become a 'brand journalist', one whose prestige goes beyond the fate and reputation of his publication. (*Libération*, in early 2014, went through another of many crises when the editor, Nicolas Demorand, attempted to turn the paper into a social network, providing content for multimedia platforms and turning the paper's offices into a cultural centre. The shareholders supported the plan, the staff rebelled.) His personality is 'a currency in the attention economy'.[1] He provides a lens through which EU affairs become understandable and, eventually, a compelling read, one which is able to spark a reflection and a debate. He is very opinionated, but people know what he stands for, and the fact that he is filming some documentaries for Arte about the EU proves that the 'Quatremer' brand works even without the *Libération* brand. He has written several respected books about the EU, he is a keen guest on TV and radio talk shows, and his passionate coverage of Belgian politics managed to foster his image as an outsider of the Euro-bubble.

His loud voice makes him recognisable even at a distance, and his solid track record of critical articles against the Commission puts him on a higher level in the Europhile vs. Eurosceptics debate, one where criticisms are just as lively as the political engagement. This does not mean that there are no controversies about his work, on the contrary. 'After 20 years here, I am detested by everyone,' he says with a certain pride. 'On the danger of being a prisoner' of the European institutions 'I would say that either you are a journalist or you are not' and the crucial thing is 'that you have to be independent: if I find something good, I write it'. He does not think his personal beliefs have to be left outside his reporting. 'I am quite liberal, but many of my colleagues, who write on the economic pages of *Libération*, are leftists, very pro-State, they don't like capitalism.'

Quatremer is a firm believer in the fact that experience plays a crucial part in understanding EU affairs. In his view Anglo-Saxon newspapers like the *FT* and *Wall Street Journal* don't grasp the huge political will on which the European project rests. 'I'm sorry to say that the Anglo-Saxon media manipulate information,' he says, pointing out that inexperienced journalists often write things 'that are obvious to everyone' because they do not have the time to learn the functioning of the EU. 'I don't say my colleagues here know nothing, but they lack depth', in his view. 'They only speak English'.

Appendix 3

The Ill-Matched Couple: TV and the EU – Hughes Beaudouin, LC1/TF1

Few journalists think that Brussels is swarming with brilliant talking heads. Eloquence, one of the most sought-after qualities for TV journalists, is often relegated to behind the scenes, and it is hard to find someone willing to explain on the record in a concise manner the complicated decisions which are taken there.

Television reporting of the EU – as of much else – differs from print-based reporting in newspapers, magazines, and on the internet most strongly in the ways in which the information is conveyed, and in the much greater pressure exerted on TV news channels, and thus on their editors and reporters, by a public whose main source of information about public affairs is television: the case throughout most of the world, and certainly in the EU. Europeans on average watch 200 minutes of TV a week: and though patterns of viewing are changing as younger generations switch to viewing on computer screens, tablets, and phones, TV news has retained a strong grip on public attention so far.

As we have noted in the main body of this text, complexity is the inevitable result of a series of institutions which are largely unfamiliar to most Europeans, which are hard to explain even in journals aimed at the highly educated – see the comment by the *Die Zeit* correspondent Matthias Krupa, that the EU is 'much more complex [than covering national politics in Germany] because of the numbers of institutions, the 28 countries, the divisions of power' and thus the correspondent 'can only give an idea, nothing like the full picture'.

Television, even the German public service networks, ZDF and ARD, giving by common consent the fullest TV coverage of the EU, cannot address this: the bulk of the viewing public won't watch it. A more polemically charged parliament will redress that balance, and give broadcasters material more suited to the dramatic needs of TV journalism: but it will do little to focus attention on the policy challenges facing the EU.

Thus, as we've seen in the case of Chris Morris, the European Correspondent of the BBC, much of the job is a search for slivers of European or EU life which have a narrative shape and can illuminate an ongoing story. Some, such as riots in Athens, have their own intrinsic watchability: others need to be constructed. Beaudouin, the Brussels-based correspondent for the French TV channel LC1, a part of the most popular channel for news, TF1, unassumingly describes his job as a constant quest for experts. 'I am a journalist, I am an expert in finding experts,' he says, describing the very strict working routine he has had for the last eight years: one daily programme at 6 a.m., which lasts for 10 minutes, and another one on Thursday evenings at 6 p.m. 'Plus, there are a lot of political talk shows on French TV and they are often about the EU, so I am asked to react to something said by a politician,' he explains.

With such intense coverage of the EU, assuring a variety of topics is of the utmost importance. 'In the morning I cover one subject – it is a discussion between me and a journalist based in Paris who asks 7–8 questions', while in the evening he does '5 or 6 subjects of 2 minutes each'. He tries to make sure the topics are diverse, that at least one is a story from the EU Parliament, and that they 'are all subjects which are not generally treated by others'. Beaudouin tries to give an insider view of Brussels by 'putting in something I picked up in the corridors – how this or that decision was taken – then something more technical, and sometimes a story which is a bit more sexy'.

Interviews and talking heads are crucial in his attempt to bring to life the often very technical stories coming from Brussels. 'The decision-making system here is hard to explain to the French', because of the differences from their own decision-making system. 'The president decides and the parliament validates', while 'in Brussels there are many powers which balance each other and must negotiate all the time'. This makes the EU system possibly easier to grasp for the Germans, but French viewers are nevertheless very interested in what happens in Brussels, even though their interest is very focused on some specific sectors.

For the French audience the European Union means first and foremost the funding of agriculture. The most expensive EU policy is notoriously divisive, but it enjoys a wide support in the Hexagone. As the leading network of the country, TF1 – of which LCI is part – has 13 million people watching its evening news and is particularly strong outside Paris. 'Issues about agriculture, such as the dispute with the Brits on support, are important for them,' he stresses. 'When Cameron said "agriculture is finished" for the people in the countryside it was a catastrophe, as 60% of their income comes from the European Commission,' he points out, adding that the future of the sector 'is much more important than the euro' for French people.

The same applies to immigration. 'It plays very strongly in the countryside, much less in Paris, which is a multicultural, multiethnic city,' says Beaudouin. 'Immigration became a much bigger subject during the crisis, and it wasn't so much before', he says, pointing out that the overall bad economic situation 'forced the issue of immigration into the open'. When a politician makes strong declarations like the Prime Minister Manuel Valls did last October (when Interior Minister), saying that Roma people are inherently 'different' and 'will have to return to Bulgaria and Romania', it is the Brussels correspondent's task to point out that it would be against EU law. Beaudouin finds it challenging to 'explain the politics here as they are without appearing to be the spokesperson for the EU', for instance when it comes to the Schengen agreement allowing the free circulation of citizens. 'I said that it was not possible, that the agreement had been signed for years [and] people told me that I had sold myself to the European Commission because I said this or that'.

A self-defined Euro-realist, Beaudouin tries to provide his audience with a multi-faceted approach to the EU. In his view the rise of Euroscepticism is mainly due to the fact that 'there has not really been a debate or an explanation of the EU in France for 50 years'. Inevitably, 'now that the politics of the EU has become an internal affair the French are asking more and more questions' and journalists have to be ready to feed the public with all the elements they need to shape their own opinion.

France is possibly the country where the two factions concerning the EU are the most vocal: on one hand the rejection of the EU Constitutional Treaty in 2005 and the impressive advance of the Front National show how unconvinced French voters are, but on the other hand the national received wisdom concerning the EU is still very respectful and takes the project very seriously. 'The French see the EU as a big France.'

Thanks to the economic crisis, 'the EU has become a matter of political debate', and the wider public is interested in what is going on. 'The Polish plumber is both a menace and an advantage,' says Beaudouin, referring to the most iconic figure among the French fears concerning the

EU and the free circulation of labour. Now people know that 'if they want their garden done for half the cost, there will be Poles offering cheaper prices'. This is a confusing situation, reckons the French journalist, one that needs to be explained properly in order to have it accepted or rejected.

But is it the only task of an EU reporter? Or is acting as a watchdog of the EU institutions part of the work of an accurate correspondent? With his trademark realism, Beaudouin points out that 'when things are going in one direction it is hard to go against it', as in the case of Greek governments having cooked the books and lied on the true state of their public finances for years.

The mutual dependence between countries makes it quite hard to denounce the wrongdoings of one. 'If we said – we made a mistake letting the Greeks in, we'll carry on feeding them, others will say another country is worse, like Italy, and what do you do then? I don't think you could have known in 2004 that the Greek debt and the Greek lying about it would have caused all this trouble.'

Appendix 4

The Rape of Europa: Anglophone Bulls in the EU China Shop – Wolfgang Blau

Of the world's 25 top online news sites, 11 are based in China, 11 in North America and three in the UK. None are in Continental Europe – though with 500 million people, mostly with relatively high incomes, Europe is the world's largest market.

The issue 'haunts' Wolfgang Blau, head of digital at the *Guardian*, as he told the annual journalism festival in Perugia in May 2014. It haunts him not because he is making an anti-American or anti-Anglophone point: he welcomes their media in Europe and works for one. But he thinks they're far too tightly focused in their coverage and misrepresent the reality of Europe, especially its cultural breadth.

It haunts him because he believes that the newspapers, websites, and wire services which cover Europe most and which play the largest part in representing it to the world at large have in the main a narrow and dispiriting agenda. Instancing the *FT*, the *Wall Street Journal, The Economist*, the *International New York Times,* and the wire services Reuters and Bloomberg, he says they are too tightly focused on the economy and have little interest in European culture.

His own view of the European Union is very broad. Speaking in Italy, he first instanced Dante's fourteenth-century vision of a united Europe – and continued through William Penn in the seventeenth century, Immanuel Kant in the eighteenth century, and Giuseppe Mazzini in the nineteenth century. These men, he said, all had a vision of a Europe peacefully united, long before the vision took on concrete form after the Second World War gave it an impetus as the mechanism that would end all intra-European wars.

Dante's vision, laid out in *De Monarchia,* is a sublime one – but also liberal, proposing a separation between church and state with toleration of all religions, including Islam. Penn, the founder of Pennsylvania and a Quaker, saw a united Europe as a mechanism for ending wars between its states – as did Immanuel Kant, who, in considering the options of a loose gathering of independent nation states with a general agreement to cooperate, or all united under one government, or a federal state with the nations as the semi-autonomous states under a federal government, plumped for the last of these as most likely to secure peace. Mazzini, the inspirer of Italians for national unity against Austrian imperial rule, transposed that aspiration for independence into a rising of all the peoples of Europe against despotism and monarchy, ending in the creation of a united state.

The Eurobarometer surveys have, since the mid-1970s, shown at best moderate liking for the 'European Union', but considerable enthusiasm for 'Europe' and a desire from those polled to know more about its culture, society, and personalities. Most thought it would be a good idea to have more integration – in strong contrast, he said, with the trend of the Anglophone European coverage.

Blau believes that national news organisations are 'over-invested in the concept of the national state' and underinvested in the development of Europe. He noted that several took the name of 'nation' in some form – *El Pais, La Nacion, Svenska Dagbladet, La Repubblica*. The news organisations which take a global view, based as they are in the US and the UK, are decisive in the creation of the image of Europe. The trend is continuing – as the news sites Huffington Post, Buzzfeed, and Vice expand into Europe – not because they have a specific European strategy, but because they have a global one, into which Europe is fitted.

These organisations have the large advantage of being Anglophone in a world where English is ever more securely the global lingua franca: but in a continent where, he said, some 50% of the population 'can have an English conversation' (that sounds too high), it should be possible to have a continental medium which could challenge the Anglo-Americans. Public broadcasters, even where generously funded – such as the BBC, with over £3bn annual income from the licence fee; or German public TV, ARD and ZDF, with over €7bn a year spent on their output – could not make up the deficit.

He conceded the failures – most obviously *The European*, Robert Maxwell's venture which closed after a few years; and said he did not have a plan in mind for a viable business model. There was, though, a journalistic imperative: the *Guardian's* revelations from the US National Security

Agency files leaked by the former NSA contractor Edward Snowden were better supported by news organisations on the continent, than in the UK. Greater European unity could see more of this solidarity.

Blau quoted the famed phrase of the nineteenth-century Count Metternich, Austrian Foreign Minister, 1809–48, foe of Mazzini, to the effect that Italy was 'a geographical expression' but which, when used politically by 'ideologues', was 'full of dangers for the very existence of the states which make up the peninsula'. He wrote that in a letter a year before the nationalist revolts forced him from office: those who believe that Europe is in an analogous position, Blau said, will be seen to be as flawed in their reasoning as Metternich, and in similar danger of loss of office.

Blau's was a case more normative than objective; not a business proposition, more a lament that Continental Europe had not summoned the political and entrepreneurial will to launch a viable publication in some form. It was encased in a view that the Anglo-Saxon media were getting it wrong – too prone to pessimism about the future of the euro, even the Union itself; and too narrow in their interests.

This case – we have quoted some adherents of it in the main text – has a wide resonance, at least among journalists and likely more widely. One of the themes of this piece has been that the overwhelming majority of the stories published by the news media on the EU are angled to show what the initiative or policy means for the country of origin of the news medium. Blau is appealing for someone – a corporation, a website, an adventurous individual – to raise the game, and express a spirit of Europe which most Anglo-Americans don't share, or share only weakly.

Ironically, the organisation best placed to attempt this is British, and Blau's employer. The *Guardian* has the name, the audience – 12 million in Europe who log into the website each month – the language, and the flair to construct a website which could mix comment, wit, cultural features, investigations with news to make up a potentially attractive package. It so far hasn't chosen to do so: it has established large offices in the US and in Australia, and – though it has a large war chest from the partial sale of the profitable *Autotrader* – still has large annual losses.

But Blau is right. There is a gap. How big the market is only a leap in the dark will tell.

Appendix 5

The Vision Betrayed: Democracy's Deficit – Dirk Schuemer

Dirk Schuemer has been, over the years, among the most enthusiastic federalists among European commentators. His platform, the feuilleton section of the *Frankfurter Algemeine Zeitung (FAZ)*, gives his voice reach and influence: and over the past few years, that voice has radically altered. His writing now is deeply disillusioned – to the point where, though a believer still in the idea and aim of a United Europe, he no longer believes that the European Union can be the vehicle for it.

Like many forceful commentators, he is inconsistent – once seeing a return to the nation state as the only exit from the EU cul-de-sac, more recently pinning hopes in a revived Parliament able to extend democratic reach to the EU and thus revive the vision by giving it a civic underpinning.

In the first register, in a column in the *FAZ* in June – written in what seemed like the endgame period for the euro – he despairs of a common vision, seeing the nations of Europe as mouthing Europhile platitudes while reinforcing national differences. No wonder: the European citizen has witnessed the growth of European power over the past few decades without ever having been asked for an opinion on it. And no common discourse has evolved:

> the EU proves that democracy can never succeed without a common discourse. *The supranational European Parliament, which in any case has hardly anything to say, is appointed in national elections. But the nightly news, the political leaders, the cultures of debate and the traditions remain purely national. Because of this, left and right majorities regularly vote against all incumbent parties when it comes to greater Europe. Here the majority of the polyglot and internationally networked elite simply holds no sway.*

A column in June 2012 sees Europe's political parties as having degenerated into purblind machines for promising benefits with money they no longer have:

> and so the political life of an organisation once built on solidarity and integration is degenerating into a contest of grasping populists and blackmailers: Europe as the front garden of a pensioner who will defend his little plot by force if need be. Once powerful movements like the Social Democrats are already intellectually and morally washed up in Italy and Greece because they have degenerated into little more than clientele groups for trade unionists and civil servants, while the needs of immigrants, youth, the unemployed and the uneducated have vanished entirely from the focus of the sated Left.

In an interview with us in April 2014, Schuemer said that

> the idea of a united Europe was the best one since the Emperor Augustus – and it's still a good idea. But you can destroy an idea by putting it into reality in the wrong way. I see the way in which the EU is being widened and deepened as being the wrong way.
>
> The most important thing is the famous democratic deficit. There has been a sort of coup d' état at the centre. The states of the union have halted any further progress. There is no parliamentary control – no voice of the people – even the senior bureaucrats agree with this. The situation is not hopeless, but it is desperate.

Schuemer says he has become sceptical about the euro currency, seeing it as a means of division rather than unity.

> I am euro sceptic rather than Eurosceptic. The euro is a very strange instrument. There is no democratic control over it – and it can ruin economies in the south. This makes me and others sceptical in a particular way – sceptical about how it can ever work. Italy can't pay back its debts.
>
> The people who preside over this, however, pay no attention to what's happening on the ground. They are like Eric Honecker [the former leader of East Germany before unification in 1990] in the 1980s, when communism was collapsing and he didn't see it. So he simply seemed silly.

His view of German media is also mordant:

> *You have two sorts of journalists, especially in Germany. One is called ideological; the other I call meteorological. The ideologists think that the EU should exist and hope it will exist and grow closer – and so they do not want to look at what is happening. I have written this for some time and the ideologists get angry with me. Daniel Cohn Bendit [the German Green politician who is a prominent MEP] insults and shouts and screams at me that I am a right winger and that I understand nothing.*
>
> *But I prefer the meteorological approach – the one you take when you look at the weather, to see if it will be a good day for a picnic tomorrow. You have to look at reality. It's the meteorological people who have been the most critical – because they see what's happening. The ideologists just go Europe – Europe – Europe. You can't take that view when you look around. I have just been to the south of Italy, and it is terrible; there is no hope there. And if we continue with the ideological approach we will ruin whatever good there is in the EU now.*

He does, however, have renewed hope in the future – seeing a real debate on the future of Europe in the Parliament prompted by the access of many more fully Eurosceptic parties, and also by what he believes is a revolt against the European leaders' habit of choosing a weak head of the Commission or the European Council – 'the Finnish Prime Minister or some such – you get Barroso – van Rompuy – Ashton. They picked them as the so-called "leaders" because the national heads of government wouldn't have anyone else.'

There are now MEPS, including the German social democrat Martin Schulz, the Parliament's president, who, Schuemer believes,

> *are angry about the powers of the national leaders. They want a functioning and democratically based transnational system. They want what we have already to work.*
>
> *A strong Eurosceptic contingent [... means that] the people will be able to speak at last. What people like me hope for – that is, a closer integration of Europe – will come through conflict.*
>
> *You need this kind of debate to convince the people of Europe of the utility of the EU. No British or German voter is presently interested in*

who is appointed the commissioner for enlargement, or the chairman of a parliamentary commission on the budget. But we are already Europeans – you realise it through struggle and through crises. You don't realise it when it works – so what a real debate gives us is a chance to understand the continent.

Appendix 6

The Cost of Communicating

To communicate its activities to over 509 million citizens from 28 member states in 24 languages, the European Commission has earmarked €246m in total for 2014. This represents a little less than 0.2% of the EU budget and the overall figure includes stakeholder communication, information for the general public and for schools, support for debates about the EU, and publications with bare facts on the EU law.

According to the 2014 budget, €66m go to the salaries of officials and temporary agents and an additional €16m are for the salaries for those tasked with press relations in the representation offices of the EU outside Brussels. There are 40 spokespersons for the European Commission – the only ones entitled to speak in the name of the institution – and each one has or shares with one other an assistant: the overall workforce of the spokespersons' office is about a hundred people. Each commissioner has at least one person dealing with the press in his or her native country.

Some communication costs are shared between the different institutions. For instance, Europe by Satellite is the EU TV information service, aimed at providing audiovisual material from the European Parliament, the European Council, the European Central Bank, the Committee of Regions, and the European Court of Justice. It is managed by the European Commission and gives live coverage of the main press conferences and briefings taking place of those institutions. The total cost indicated in the Commission budget for 2014 is €5.324m, including the expenses for renting the satellite allowing the two channels EbS and EbS+ to be seen all over Europe, in North Africa, and in the Middle East.

The Parliament has its own EuroparlTV, which costs €5m per year according to the 2014 budget. The EU Parliament also spends €15.6m for 'audiovisual information', namely the broadcasting of meetings and sessions, for creating its own TV programmes and for securing citizens' access to the archives. The Commission does not own the news channel Euronews – a common belief – but does contribute some €15m to its €60m annual budget.

Communication in the Parliament is less easy to track, since each of the 751 MEPs has at least one person dealing with the press, even though it might not be his only task. The 2014 budget earmarks €21.036m per year to finance its communication activities, including PR and printing of information for the public. The spokespersons' office of the Parliament has about 26 people, plus a press officer for each member state and a representative in 30 EU cities: it totals 86 persons dealing with the communication of the Parliament.

The Council has a slightly larger team, about 100 people, including technicians and photographers, and 10 persons dedicated to monitoring the press. The total budget of the Council for 2014 is €534.2m and the total costs earmarked for information are €10.4m, of which less than half is strictly dedicated to communication.

Notes

All online resources last accessed May 2014.

Chapter 1   Introduction: Feast and Famine

1 Hans Magnus Enzensberger, *Brussels, the Gentle Monster or the Disenfranchisement of Europe* (Seagull, 2011), 8.

Chapter 2   The Limits of Utopia: Leaving Loyalty, Embracing Scepticism

1 Olivier Baisnée, Thomas Frinault, and Bleuwenn Lechaux, 'The Case of France', in AIM Research Consortium (ed.), *Understanding the Logic of EU Reporting from Brussels* (ProjektVerlag, 2007), 40.
2 Ibid., 40.
3 Ibid.
4 Riccardo Perissich, *L'Unione europea, una storia non ufficiale* (Longanesi, 2008), 291.
5 Paul Collowald, 'C'est la faute à Bruxelles', *La Cité*, 2 June 1994.
6 'The hitherto foreign correspondence out of Brussels or Strasbourg concerning European decision-making has turned into much more of an integrative performance.' Gerd G. Kopper, 'Research and the Meta-Level of Practice: Implications for Training, Online Communicating and Defining Rules of European Journalism', in AIM Research Consortium (ed.), *Reporting and Managing European News* (ProjektVerlag, 2007), 195.
7 Margaret Thatcher, Speech to the College of Europe, 'Bruges Speech', 20 Sept. 1988.
8 Jean-Michel Demetz, Jean-Marie Pontaut, François Geoffroy, and Fabrice Lhomme, 'L'affaire Cresson, complot ou scandale à Bruxelles?', *Le Nouvel Observateur*, 11 Mar. 1999.
9 Daniel C. Hallin and Paolo Mancini, *Comparing Media Systems: Three Models of Media and Politics* (Cambridge University Press, 2004).
10 Ibid., 251ff. See also Henrik Örnebring, *Comparative European Journalism: The State of Current Research*, Reuters Institute for the Study of Journalism, working paper, Jan. 2009.

11 The treaty, signed in the Dutch city in Feb. 1992, brought the European Union formally into being, paved the way for a single currency, and set criteria for the convergence of the economies of the EU members.

12 Kopper, 'Research and the Meta-Level of Practice', in AIM Research Consortium, *Reporting and Managing*, 187–8.

13 This figure is probably too high: the BBC has no readily available figures, but says that many reporters would come to Brussels for a particular story or set of stories, though would not be based there.

Chapter 3   Communicating to the Communicators: How the EU Presents Itself

1 Olivier Baisnée, 'Understanding EU News Production Logics: Norms, Channels and Structures of Reporting Europe from Brussels', in AIM Research Consortium, *Reporting and Managing*, 26.

2 Andy Smith (ed.), *Politics and the European Commission: Actors, Interdependence, Legitimacy* (Routledge, 2004).

3 Olivier Baisnée, 'The Politics of the Commission as an Informative Source', in Smith, *Politics and the European Commission*, 134.

4 Guy Georges, 'De l'art de communiquer', *Le Monde*, 29 Jan. 1999. Reicherts goes on to say: 'We have, I think, to involve the API (International Press Association) and make it more responsible in this evolution. Explain that some excesses took place [...] Draw a list of clear misinformation cases (there are many!). Let them understand that they don't have anything to earn from this "corrida" atmosphere. [...] We have to reflect on the very notion of "transparence": not being obsessed with it, not trying to be "more catholic than the king". A certain dose of cynicism – and sometimes of hypocrisy – in the way we spread information is sometimes necessary. Aiming at explaining everything and setting oneself as a model of completeness often triggers new questioning. Over information often borders with disinformation [...] Therefore we have to learn to freeze part of the information where we are not completely sure, where we know it could be misinterpreted. With some journalists, particularly twisted, we have to accept sadly that we need to make some violence to ourselves.'

5 In its 2014 budget, the EU Council earmarked €2.2m, i.e. £1.8m, for information and public events: http://eur-lex.europa.eu/budget/data/LBL2014/EN/SEC02.pdf, p. 23.

6 Julia Hobsbawm (ed.), *Where the Truth Lies* (Atlantic Books, 2006), 5.

Chapter 4   Growing Apart: The Argument over Objectivity

1 'The remarkable rise of continental Euroscepticism', *The Guardian*, 24 Apr. 2013: www.theguardian.com/commentisfree/2013/apr/24/continental-euroscepticism-rise.

2 John Lloyd and Ferdinando Giugliano, *Eserciti di Carta* (Feltrinelli, 2013), 9–10.

3   A comprehensive account of the Italian press in Brussels is found in Alessio Cornia, *Notizie da Bruxelles: Logiche e problemi della costruzione giornalistica a Bruxelles* (FrancoAngeli, 2010).

4   Edith Cresson, Prime Minister of France in the early 1990s, then sent to be the European Commissioner for research and education, was at the centre of a fraud which caused the Santer administration to resign. A fraud inquiry set up by the Commission found that she 'failed to act in response to known, serious and continuing irregularities over several years'. She was found guilty of not reporting failures in a youth training programme from which vast sums went missing, and of showing favouritism in hiring her dentist as an AIDS expert in 1995. The man was later judged to be unqualified and his work was deemed to be grossly deficient. She did not, however, gain personally from her actions, the report said.

5   Paul Statham, 'Making Europe News: How Journalists View their Role and Media Performance', *Journalism*, 9/4, 398–422, here 415.

6   Independent panel report, *BBC Coverage of the European Union*, Jan. 2005:   http://downloads.bbc.co.uk/bbctrust/assets/files/pdf/our_work/govs/independentpanelreport.pdf, p. 3.

7   Ibid., 4–5.

8   Ibid., 5.

9   Ibid., 7.

10   'The European Union: Perceptions of the BBC's Reporting. Management's Response', May 2005: http://downloads.bbc.co.uk/bbctrust/assets/files/pdf/our_work/govs/eu_management_response.pdf, p. 2.

11   Jan Hornát, 'A reflection on Czech Euroscepticism before the EU elections', 16 Jan. 2014: www.opendemocracy.net/can-europe-make-it/jan-hornát/reflection-on-czech-euroscepticism-before-eu-elections.

Chapter 5   The Limits: The EU from 'Dull' to 'Crucial' in a Time of Crisis

1   David Marsh, *Europe's Deadlock* (Yale University Press, 2013), 111.

2   Ibid.

Chapter 6   Living in Financial Times: Getting to Grips with Financial Complexity

1   Vangelis Demeris, *La face cachée de la crise grecque* (La Boîte à Pandore, 2012).

2   Stephen Gray and Dina Kyriakidou, 'Special Report: Greece's Triangle of Power', 17 Dec. 2012:   http://mobile.reuters.com/article/topNews/idUSBRE8BG0CF20121217?i=2.

3   Liz Alderman, 'Greek Editor Is Arrested After Publishing a List of Swiss Bank Accounts', *New York Times*, 28 Oct. 2012: www.nytimes.com/2012/10/29/world/europe/greek-editor-arrested-after-publishing-list-of-swiss-bank-accounts.html.

4 Christos Ziotis and Marcus Bensasson, 'Greece Targeting Tax Dodgers Seeks UK Model From Swiss', 4 Feb. 2014: www.bloomberg.com/news/2014-02-04/greece-seeks-deal-on-swiss-secret-funds-as-tax-dodgers-targeted.html.

Chapter 7   Video Games: The Challenges for TV Journalists and the Role of 'Mass' Media

1 Paschal Preston, *Making the News* (Routledge, 2009), 155.
2 Ibid., 156.
3 Pierre Bourdieu, *Sur la télévision* (Raisons d'Agir, 1996), 13.
4 Ivo Mosley (ed.), *Not so Dumb in Dumbing Down* (Imprint Academic, 2000), 171.
5 Philip Thomasson-Lerulf and Hannes Kataja, *The European Union's Burden: Information and Communication to a Reluctant People* (Timbro, July 2009).

Chapter 8 Absent Enemies: Reporting on Brussels out of Brussels

1 Charles Grant, *Delors: Inside the House that Jacques Built* (Nicholas Brearley, 1994).
2 Andrew Gimson, *Boris* (Simon & Schuster, 2012), 104.
3 'Euromyths and Letters to the Editor': http://ec.europa.eu/unitedkingdom/blog/index_en.htm.

Chapter 9   The Globalists: Reporting for the Elite

1 Pierre Manent, 'Birth of the Nation', *City Journal,* Winter 2013: www.city-journal.org/2013/23_1_nation-state.html.
2 Preston, *Making the News.*

Chapter 10   Dog Does Eat Dog: Peer Pressure and Peer Reviews

1 Thilo Sarrazin, *Deutschland schafft sich ab* (DVA, 2010).
2 Thilo Sarrazin, *Deutschland braucht den Euro nicht* (DVA, 2012).
3 On the case of Bettina Schulz, see also Ulrike Simon, 'Vor Gericht: Faz streit sich mit langjahriger Korrespondentin', *Newsroom,* 12. Feb 2013: www.newsroom.de/news/detail/777434; and Martin Kotynek, 'Endstation Frankfurt?', *Die Zeit,* 15 Apr. 2013: www.zeit.de/2013/15/faz-korrespondentin-versetzung.
4 The *Wall Street Journal*'s story on its own circulation, written on 14 October 2011 (the *Guardian*'s story was on 12 October) claims 'fewer than 11,000 papers [...] sold at 50 per cent or more of the full price'. The Dutch company Executive Learning Partnership bought the *Journal* in bulk for one European cent a copy, and distributed them to students in various European universities. The paper's European publisher, Andrew Langhoff, resigned after an internal inquiry found that he had attempted to pressurise his editorial colleagues into running favourable stories on the Dutch company.

Chapter 11   Tweeting into Clarity: Online is Demanding, But Helpful

1 C. W. Anderson, Emily Bell, and Clay Shirky, *Post Industrial Journalism: Adapting to the Present* (Columbia Journalism School, 2012): http://towcenter. org/research/post-industrial-journalism.

Appendix 1   Euroscepticism: Boris Johnson and Bruno Waterfield

1 Gimson, *Boris* (1st edn, 2006).
2 Tony Judt, *Postwar* (Penguin, 2005).
3 Bruno Waterfield, 'The EU wants powers to sack journalists', 22 Jan. 2013: www.telegraph.co.uk/news/uknews/leveson-inquiry/9817625/Leveson-EU-wants-power-to-sack-journalists.html.
4 The members of the group were Professor Vaira Vike-Freiberga, a linguistic scholar whose work had specialised in memory processes and language: she had been elected as President of Latvia, serving 1999–2007; Professor Herta Daubler-Gmelin, a legal scholar, former SPD MP and former German Federal Justice Minister: she resigned following publication of a remark she made in 2002 in what she thought was a private meeting, to the effect that President George W. Bush was preparing for war in Iraq to deflect attention from the US economic crisis, and that was a strategy followed by Hitler; Ben Hamersley, Innovator in Residence at the Centre for Creative and Social Technologies at Goldsmiths College, University of London and an editor at large for *Wired Magazine*; and Professor Luis Miguel Poiares Pessoa Maduro, director of the Global Governance Programme at the European University Institute in Florence and a professor in the department of law in the New University of Lisbon.

Appendix 2   The Passionate Chronicler: Jean Quatremer

1 Saska Saarikoski, *Brands, Stars and Regular Hacks: A Changing Relationship between News Institutions and Journalists* (Reuters Institute for the Study of Journalism, 2012).

Bibliography

AIM Research Consortium, *Understanding the Logic of EU Reporting in Mass Media: Analysis of EU Media Coverage and Interviews in Editorial Offices in Europe* (ProjektVerlag, 2006).

AIM Research Consortium, *Reporting and Managing European News: Final Report of the Project 'Adequate Information Management in Europe', 2004–2007* (ProjektVerlag, 2007).

AIM Research Consortium, *Understanding the Logic of EU Reporting from Brussels: Analysis of Interviews with EU Correspondents and Spokespersons* (ProjektVerlag, 2007).

Anderson, C. W., Bell, E., and Shirky, C., *Post Industrial Journalism: Adapting to the Present* (Columbia Journalism School, 2012).

Azrout, R., Spanje, J. van, and Vreese, C. H. de, 'When News Matters: Media Effects on Public Support for EU Enlargement in 21 Countries', *Journal of Common Market Studies*, 50 (2012), 691–708.

Baisnée, O., 'Can Political Journalism Exist at the EU Level?', in R. Kuhn and E. Neveu (eds), *Political Journalism: New Challenges, New Practices* (Routledge, 2002), 108–28.

Baisnée, O., 'La production de l'actualité communautaire: Elements d'une sociologie comparee du corps de presse (France, Grande Bretagne)', doctoral dissertation, Université de Rennes, 2003.

Baisnée, O., 'En être ou pas: Les logiques de l'entre soi à Bruxelles', *Actes de la Recherche en Sciences Sociales*, 166 (2007), 110–21.

Baisnée, O., 'The European Public Sphere Does Not Exist (At Least it's Worth Wondering …)', *European Journal of Communication*, 22/4 (2007), 493–503.

Baisnée, O., 'A Sociology of the European Media and EU Journalism', in Adrian Favell and Virginie Guiraudon (eds), *Sociology of the European Union* (Palgrave Macmillan, 2012).

Berger, H., Ehrmann, M., and Fratzscher, M., *Monetary Policy in the Media* (Centre for Economic Policy Research, 2011).

Boomgaarden, H. G., et al., 'Mapping EU Attitudes: Conceptual and Empirical Dimensions of Euroskepticism and EU Support', *European Union Politics*, 12/2 (2011), 241–66.

Bourdieu, P., *Sur la télévision* (Raisons d'Agir, 1996).

Carey, S., and Burton, J., 'The Influence of the Press in Shaping Public Opinion towards the European Union in Britain', *Political Studies*, 52/3 (2004), 623–40.

Chalaby, J., 'Transnational Television in Europe: The Role of Pan-European Channels', *European Journal of Communication*, 17/2 (2002), 183–203.

Chalaby, J., 'Deconstructing the Transnational: A Typology of Cross-Border Television Channels in Europe', *New Media and Society*, 7/2 (2005), 155–75.

Cornia, A., *Notizie da Bruxelles. Logiche e problemi della costruzione giornalistica dell'Unione europea* (FrancoAngeli, 2011).

Dassetto, F., and Dumoulin, M., *Naissance et developpement de l'information européenne* (Euroclio/Peter Lang, 1993), 119–32.

Downey, J., and Koenig, T., 'Is there a European Public Sphere? The Berlusconi–Schultz Case', *European Journal of Communication*, 21/2 (2006), 165–87.

Enzensberger, H. M., *Brussels the Gentle Monster or the Disenfrenchisement of Europe* (Seagull, 2011).

Eriksen, E. O., and Fossum, J. E., *Democracy in the European Union: Integration through Deliberation?* (Routledge, 2000).

European Journal of Communication, Special issue on 'The media and European public space', 22/4 (Dec. 2007).

Frank, R., et al., *Building the European Public Sphere: History and the Global Perspective* (P.I.E. Peter Lang, 2010).

Gavin, N. T., 'Imagining Europe: Political Identity and British Television Coverage of the European Union', *British Journal of Politics and International Relations*, 2/3 (2000), 352–73.

Gehrke, G., *Europe without the Europeans: A Question of Communication?* (European Institute for the Media, 1998).

Gimson, A., *Boris* (Simon & Schuster, 2012).

Gleissner, M., and Vreese, C. H. de, 'News about the EU Constitution: Journalistic Challenges and Media Portrayal of the European Union Constitution', *Journalism*, 6/2 (2005), 221–42.

Grant, C., *Inside the House that Jacques Built* (Nicholas Brearly, 1994).

Gyngell, K., and Keighley, D., *An Outbreak of Narcolepsy? Why the BBC Must Improve its Coverage of the EU* (Center for Policy Studies, 2004).

Hallin, D. C., and Mancini, P., *Comparing Media Systems: Three Models of Media and Politics* (Cambridge University Press, 2004).

Harrison, J., and Wessels, B. (eds), *Mediating Europe: New Media, Mass Communications and the European Public Sphere* (Berghahn Books, 2012).

Inthorn, S., *German Media and National Identity* (Cambria Press, 2007).

Judt. T., *Postwar* (Penguin, 2005).

Kevin, D., *Europe in the Media: A Comparison of Reporting, Representation and Rhetoric in National Media Systems in Europe* (Erlbaum, 2003).

Koopmans, R., and Statham, P., *The Making of a European Public Sphere: Media Discourse and Political Contention* (Cambridge University Press, 2010).

Lloyd, J., and Giugliano, F., *Eserciti di Carta* (Feltrinelli, 2013).

Machill, M., 'Euronews: The First European News Channel as a Case Study for Media Industry Development in Europe and for Spectra of Transnational Journalism Research', *Media, Culture and Society*, 20/4 (1998), 427–50.

Machill, M., Beiler, M., and Fischer, C., 'Europe-Topics in Europe's Media: The Debate about the European Public Sphere. A Meta-Analysis of Media Content Analysis', *European Journal of Communication*, 21/1 (2006), 57–88.

Mancini, P., 'Is there a European Model of Journalism?', in H. de Burgh (ed.), *Making Journalists* (Routledge, 2005).

Marsh, D., *Europe's Deadlock* (Yale University Press, 2013).

Martins, A. J., Lecheler, S., and Vreese, C. H. de, 'Information Flow and Communication Deficit: Perceptions of Brussels-Based Correspondents and EU Officials', *Journal of European Integration*, 34/4 (2012), 305–22.

Mosley, I. (ed.), *Not so Dumb in Dumbing Down* (Imprint Academic, 2000).

Morgan, D., 'British Media and European Union News: The Brussels News Beat and its Problems', *European Journal of Communication*, 10/3 (1995), 321–43.

Morganti, L., and Bekemans, L. (eds), *European Public Sphere: From Critical Thinking to Responsible Action* (Peter Lang, 2011).

Örnebring, H., *Comparative European Journalism: The State of Current Research*, Reuters Institute for the Study of Journalism, working paper, Jan. 2009.

Perissich, R., *L'Unione europea, una storia non ufficiale* (Longanesi, 2008).

Preston, P., *Making the News* (Routledge, 2009).

Psychogiopoulou, E. (ed.), *Understanding Media Policies: A European Perspective* (Palgrave Macmillan, 2012).

Russ-Mohl, S., 'Towards a European Journalism? Limits, Opportunities, Challenges', *Studies in Communication Sciences*, 3/2 (2003), 203–16.

Sarrazin, T., *Deutschland schafftssich ab* (DVA, 2010).

Sarazzin, T., *Deutschland braucht den euro nicht* (DVA, 2012).

Schuck, A., and Vreese, C. H. de, 'When Good News is Bad News: Explicating the Underlying Dynamics behind the Reversed Mobilization Effect', *Journal of Communication*, 62 (2012), 57–77.

Semetko, H. A., Vreese, C. de, and Peter, J., 'Europeanised Politics – Europeanised media? European Integration and Political Communication', *West European Politics*, 23/4 (2000), 121–41.

Schlesinger, P., 'Changing Spaces of Political Communication: The Case of the European Union', *Political Communication*, 16/3 (1999), 263–79.

Smith, A. (ed.), *Politics and the European Commission: Actors, Independence, Legitimacy* (Routledge, 2004).

Statham, P., *Political Journalism and Europeanization: Pressing Europe?* (Centre for European Political Communications [Leeds], 2006).

Statham, P., 'Journalists as Commentators on European Politics: Educators, Partisans or Ideologues?', *European Journal of Communication*, 22/4 (2007), 461–77.

Statham, P., and Trenz, H. J. (eds), *Political Communication, Media and Constitution Building in Europe: The Search for a Public Sphere* (Routledge, 2010).

Statham, P., and Trenz, H. J., *The Politicization of Europe: Contesting the Constitution in the Mass Media* (Routledge, 2013).

Van Dalen, A., Albaeck, E., and Vreese, C. H. de, 'Suspicious Minds: Explaining Political Cynicism among Political Journalists in Europe', *European Journal of Communication,* 26/2 (2011), 147–62.

Vliegenthart, R., et al., 'News Coverage and Support for European Integration 1990–2006', *International Journal of Public Opinion Research,* 20/4 (2009), 415–39.

Vreese, C. H. de, *Framing Europe: Television News and European Integration* (Transaction, 2003).

RISJ/I.B.TAURIS PUBLICATIONS

CHALLENGES

Reporting the EU: News, Media and the European Institutions
John Lloyd and Cristina Marconi
ISBN: 978 1 78453 065 5

Transformations in Egyptian Journalism
Naomi Sakr
ISBN: 978 1 78076 589 1

Climate Change in the Media: Reporting Risk and Uncertainty
James Painter
ISBN: 978 1 78076 588 4

Women and Journalism
Suzanne Franks
ISBN: 978 1 78076 585 3

EDITED VOLUMES

Media and Public Shaming: The Boundaries of Disclosure
Julian Petley (ed.)
ISBN: 978 1 78076 586 0 (HB); 978 1 78076 587 7 (PB)

*Political Journalism in Transition: Western Europe in a
Comparative Perspective*
Raymond Kuhn and Rasmus Kleis Nielsen (eds)
ISBN: 978 1 78076 677 5 (HB); 978 1 78076 678 2 (PB)

*Transparency in Politics and the Media: Accountability and
Open Government*
Nigel Bowles, James T. Hamilton and David A. L. Levy (eds)
ISBN: 978 1 78076 675 1 (HB); 978 1 78076 676 8 (PB)

The Ethics of Journalism: Individual, Institutional and Cultural Influences
Wendy N. Wyatt (ed.)
ISBN: 978 1 78076 673 7 (HB); 978 1 78076 674 4 (PB)